Being Good
A Medley of Love

Dr. Phil Stack
2014

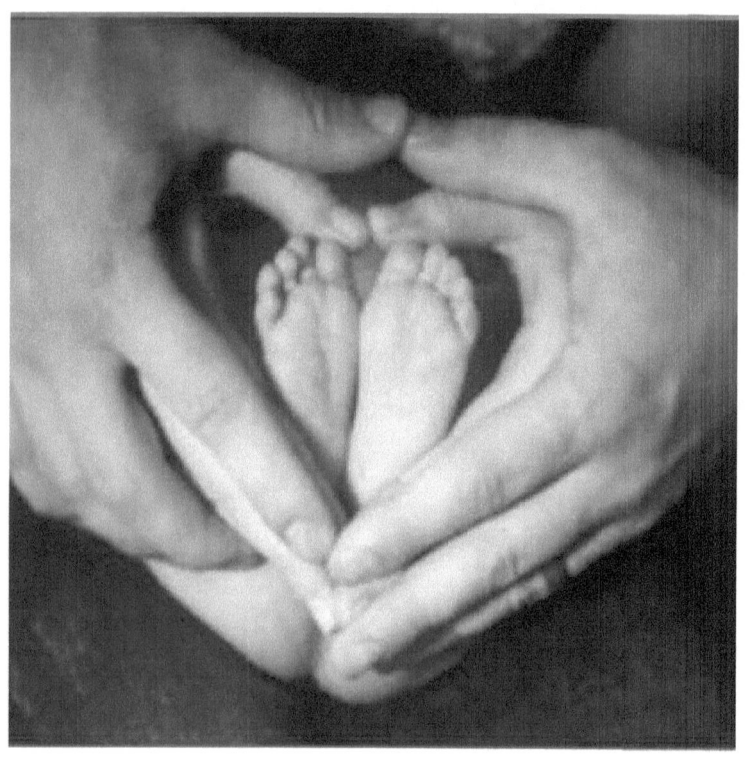

Contents

Being Good   A Medley of Love

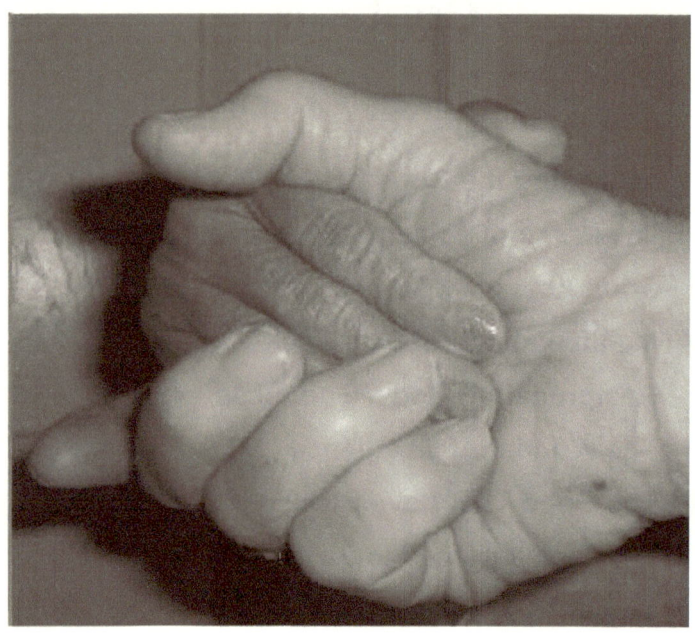

Introduction

THANK GOD FOR YOU

Of that good
God gave to you
His very best
Comes shining through

Memories are Happier
More smiles shine on every face
More love is shared heart to heart,
Just because of you.

Angels in Heaven, with joy, proclaim:
This earth will never be the same.
The Lord is pleased, rejoice each day
For you have walked
HIS BLESSED WAY.

I
Assessing the Good

Good is a word—and more. It represents a description, It is a word Applied with great ease And frequency. It is so versatile it can apply to anything, a piece of paper, a curtain, even a person.

Good is like a piece of taffy; it stretches. It doesn't cease with "good morning." It is drawn out with a "good afternoon" followed by "good evening" and the beautiful and sometimes romantic, "good night My Life" is filled with the word. There is the good neighbor, good faith, and sayings like "Good golly, Miss Molly," "The greatest good for the greatest number" *Lady be good" and "The good, the bad, and the ugly." There is the Cape of Good Hope, good fortune, Good Queen Bess, The Good Shepherd, and Goodyear Tires.

Good is an infestation. There is more good in the world than there are ants crawling in die jungles, and, I am advised by the bug people, they too are good.

Good is cross-cultural; it crosses religious boundaries, it has no sex discrimination, and it has no territorial bias. Good speaks for unity because it can be derived from everything imaginable.

Reach for the Good
in the clay and the dirt,
and build jour statue of priceless worth;
Stroke the good in coloring,
then paint the lovely birds that sing.

> *Find the good in a fallen tree,*
> *and let it shelter your family.*

Take an "o" from "good;" God is there. Good, like God, is everywhere.

The Primary Mover of All That Is Good.

At the Smithsonian in Washington, D.C there is a huge pendulum attached by a cord high up on die ceiling. Its function is to move back and forth. But who caused it to move? Just like the pendulum, the universe had a start and God made that first move. Nothing moved until He gave a first nudge. A good act is like that. It won't happen unless someone initiates it. Someone first notices a need and says, for example, "I will help build that house for the poor," or "I will share my potatoes." It follows that if you have abundant power, you can do great things. However, if you have only potatoes, then potatoes are the best you can give.

But why do we give the vegetables? Perhaps because there is hunger, and we have compassion. We may give because the crop was good, and, having more than we needed for ourselves, we share out of our abundance. We may give because we anticipate something in return or because we want to show off and give our good image a face-lift. But something is left out. When citing the various reasons for performing a good act we forgot the most significant one of all, obedience to God. We fulfill another's need not because of self-interests, which are often ruled by unbridled emotions, but because we obey God.

"Love your neighbor as yourself," is His clear directive.

When there is an observed need, we listen at two levels of obedience. First, we listen at the level of the person's need, like hunger. The condition speaks out as clearly as words. Second, we listen to God and hear, "Obey my word; feed the hungry." The belief system is with God. All guidance, therefore, for combining need with the appropriate good act, occurs with a fervent desire to obey God.

God Created Man and He Called It Very Good

When God created earth. He called it "good," and when He created man. He called him "very good." Likewise, the role of man is to convert the raw material, the changeable gifts of die earth, which are good, to a very good, self-serving, practical condition. The gift of a tree, for example, is good. However, utilizing intellect, the tree can be made into a house, which is very good. The tree can also become an object of joy and good cheer at Christmas time. An intended purpose of human beings is to strive for perfection, to be progressive, to convert what is good into a very good condition. The purpose is to improve the quality of man's life, to serve in enhancing his worth, dignity, and capacities.

In the moral sphere, God seeks from man a pursuit of unity. A quaint example is a child's drawing of a person with an arm missing. The picture is not complete. Draw an arm in the appropriate place and it becomes a unit, a total picture of a person. Consider also a man pursuing a woman. They merge into a love unit, a total composite of he and she. Their oneness is further solidified by the birth of a child.

Suppose you find a person shivering in the cold. Something is wrong with that image. It represents a need without fulfillment. But what does the need require to make right the image? Warmth. With a chivalrous gesture you offer your coat, deciding to be cold in his or her place. By adding warmth, you have completed the picture. You have established a unity, a oneness. It is not unlike the bitter cold of empty space becoming, all of a sudden, warmed by the creation of God's universe.

When a need and a good act combine, there is a sense that they were meant to come together.

What Makes You Want to Be Good?

You may want to be good because you see the proper qualities in yourself. You judge yourself to be compassionate, helpful, giving, and obedient.

You may want to be good because of the benefits you will accrue, believing in die tenet, "What goes around comes around." Furthermore, people will like you if you are good, and they will accept you for your positive qualities. They will see in you virtuous attributes: honesty, reliability, trustworthiness, and kindness. You may feel compelled to be good in order to follow an example obediently.

* * *

"Take my chair," Nancy said, seeing that I was standing. Since I was quite a bit older, she made an assessment of our mutual inconveniences and concluded that I would suffer more by standing than she. Nancy's good act was only for me. I was the direct beneficiary but I was also unknown to her, neither a friend nor a relative. I was certainly not the president or a king. Then she would be pleasing only out of courtesy and respect rather than noticing a personal need.

When a parent requests a child to do something, and the child responds obediently, just as Nancy responded to my perceived need, the obedience should please the parent because a certain amount of respect is indicated. When we respond to another person's need, we have also listened, and, by listening and providing a fulfillment, we have increased the value of the person we have helped. We can enhance a person's value with the tiniest act of goodness, or we can increase it by an overwhelming act of goodness, a good act so powerful it can be remembered always. But what person would sacrifice that much for an unknown?

Do you know of someone who will suffer for you in order to elevate your personal status, as well as the status of everyone, so all can enjoy infinite value? It would be someone who performed a good act that was magnificent, the best ever. It would be a person who would take your suffering on Himself. He would suffer not only for a single incident, but for a whole lifetime of imperfections, and He would do it in such a way that He could never be forgotten.

The grandest good act of all was Jesus dying on the cross. He was King of die universe, not merely of the world. He taught us by example to be good, that our goodness be inclusive, and that we become self-less in treating the common person as the most treasured creature of all.

When you hear from someone, "Nobody treated me so nicely in my whole life," then you have followed the example of God. Then you have increased the value of that person with a sublime good act whose impact travels to the soul's depth.

Jesus suffered a great inconvenience by dying and elevating you and me to the highest peak of a wonderful status, making us heaven-worthy just because we are persons.

I also want to be good, selfless, and inconvenienced as I increase the value of others, just as my value has been so magnificently elevated by the suffering of the Lord. That is my reason, my passion for being good.

How to Be Called a Good Person without even Trying

Consider a boy who sits beneath a plum tree. The plums have ripened, and he has made no effort to reach for a plum, yet would very much like to have one. He ponders, "How can I have it and not reach for it?" and he waits for somebody else to reach for the plum because he prefers to have it handed to him. Yet, he calls himself a plum picker. He says it because it is a favored title and everyone dislikes being called that other name, idle-sitter.

Can one deserve to be called a plum-picker while pursuing only the role of idle-sitter?

Twenty voting people, ages 14 to 18, gathered in a circle. "Are you a good person?" I asked them. Each, without hesitation, said "Yes."

Then I asked, "Why are you good persons?" Probably being group-influenced, they replied, "Because we are not bad persons." None volunteered to explain the good they do. None mentioned their kindness toward others. Instead, they accepted the label "good" without explanation, without lifting a "goodness-finger." The twenty are saying, "Don't make us accountable. Being good is not uppermost in our minds. We don't have to pick the plums because we certified ourselves as plum-pickers already. We don't have to be concerned with the responsibility of good acts because we are good already."

Apparently these children have been given the good promise, the message that God will take care of them. Indeed. God will take care of them, but they need to follow the message of God expressed through good actions. To say that one is good does not mean he does good acts.

Can You Respond to Hunger If You See It?

If you see a skinny dog you might feel he is hungry; if you see skinny dogs over and over you might feel like you're in an impoverished country. If dogs are skinny in that country you might judge that food is scarce, and, maybe, there are skinny children living there also. With all that skinniness showing you might even judge that you are in a third world country where there is much poverty.

I was in a country, driving around in a comfortable van with three children and four adults on board, where I saw an abundance of skinny dogs. I focused on the three children, ages six, nine, and twelve, because they attended a religious private school, and each child brought along a book on gospel readings.

If anyone should notice the skinny dogs and skinny, hungry kids, I was sure the children would. They did not. It did not concern them in the slightest, even when I repeated, over and over, "There goes a skinny, hungry dog."

We had a bag full of assorted candies, many more than the children could eat. "Could I have a handful of candies?" I asked. "When I see some poor children playing along the road I want to toss out some candies for them."

No response came from the children sitting in the rear of the van. But one aunt responded, "Charity begins at home," meaning the candy is not for sharing.

It was lunchtime. All four adults and three children decided on fried chicken. A whole bucket of aromatic chicken pieces—breasts, thighs, legs, and wings were soon being gobbled up by the group. I consumed four pieces along with mashed potatoes, peas, beans, and slaw. I soon began to collect the leftovers into a plastic bag for the skinny dogs.

Just as I was about to enter the van with my bag full of chicken scraps, something began tugging at my bag. I looked down to find two soiled children looking up at me. One was holding the bag and pointing to his mouth. I opened it and suddenly a tiny hand plunged inside grabbing a hand full of scraps.

"Wait," I said. "Take it all," and I handed the older, more aggressive boy, the whole bag. His sullen face brightened with a gigantic smile of joy as his skinny, dirty body writhed with excitement. Then he dashed off holding the bag, followed by three other skinny kids.

I wondered what the three children would report to their teacher regarding the trip?

Hearing What You Should Do Does Not Mean You Will Listen

If a child hears, "Love one another as I have loved you," or "Feed the hungry," what will happen? Probably nothing. The format of the preacher is to tell you what the Bible says you should do. He can preach incessantly with clarity and vigor and never know the impact on the lives of the listeners. A few compliments are offered afterwards expressing polite satisfaction, but it is an aesthetic or intellectual satisfaction, not a spirited, "Now I will do things differently." I have never seen a church where the flow of God's goodness through its members is assessed from one week to the next.

It is difficult to shift from "God will provide" to "Love thy neighbor." "God will provide" is a more popular sermon, I think. And if it brings money into the church coffers, then maybe you will hear the "God will provide" kind of sermon more regularly. Yet we should study the veracity of this issue.

The choice we have is to take or to emulate, to receive from God or to do as God does as an act of obedience. Perhaps there should be a blending of both in the same person. In difficult moments you ask for God's assistance; in strengthened times you take care of your neighbor and behave God-like toward him. If you have learned to emulate God and are inclined to disseminate God's goodness, your good acts may spread further that you would think. It is my contention that many people know that they should be good but are not entirely aware why they should be good, how to be good, when to be good, or where to be good. Therefore, they may not realize the fullest manifestations of God's goodness through them.

This book is intended to offer examples and insights that may increase the flow of God's goodness, through everyone, into a needy world.

Do You Want to Be a Good Person?

Not everyone feels they are a good person. I made two hundred buttons which read "I am a good person" and distributed them among many people. A dozen of the two hundred hesitated or refused to wear the button, saying, "Only God can make that judgment". One elderly woman refused a button because, as a child, her chores had doubled for "tooting her own horn." One refused for a completely opposite reason, announcing, "I don't need your button because everyone knows I am a good person." The vast majority accepted the button and promptly pinned it on, stating forthrightly, "Yes, I am a good person." Interestingly enough, there were quite a few who responded, "I try to be." These were willing to wear the button as a reminder to improve themselves. "I'll look at the button," remarked one store clerk, "when I need to control my temper."

Some Variations of Good Acts

Singular good acts: These acts have a simple objective. You help someone cross the street, and your good act is done. You hold the door for someone, and the good act is finished.

Multiple good acts: You do several good acts for the same person. Give him a ride, buy him food, and pay for his hotel. Here the caring is much more intensified and comprehensive. Multiple acts are not easily forgotten.

Simple or routine good acts: A smile or a "good morning" represents a simple good act. It is what we do every day. It is part of the "good manners" others expect of us. The routine good acts arc individualized. How and when one manifests them is unique to that person. Change that routine, that idiosyncrasy, and everyone notices.

Complex or sacrificial good acts: You accept refugees from another country. They cannot speak English. You feed them, buy them clothes, give them medical attention, and find them work. You help organize their lives in a new society and then allow them to journey to a place where they feel comfortable with friends.

Immediate response with good acts: These are urgent. They require emergency care, such as rushing a person to the hospital. These can also be emergency issues that arise from natural catastrophes such as earthquakes, hurricanes, tornadoes, and floods.

Future effects of good acts: Teach a child by word of mouth or by example the merits of good conduct. What good acts we perform in our families today will help strengthen the adaptive goodness quality in our children during later years.

Unilateral good acts: You perform a good act, such as giving your neighbor a basketful of your garden potatoes, and you receive no tangible item in return. The process of giving goes one way. For that reason it is not the most popular interaction involving a good act.

Reciprocated good acts: Good acts that occur with a payback are very common. You give your neighbor the potatoes, and she gives you a jar of her canned beets. In the business world reciprocation is rampant. Each time you chose to have an item or a service and you pay for it, you have reciprocated.

Manipulated good acts: Transactions can be unjust or uneven. In the manipulation process one tries to achieve a benefit or gain that is more than one is entitled to having. Deception through misrepresentation, lying, and cheating are methods of looking good by establishing an untruth about oneself. 'These are often risky endeavors because they may result in mistrust or a negative image that is difficult to alter.

Sincere or deliberate good acts: These good acts are done purposefully. For these you go out of your routine. You seek the need, like a missionary does, rather than simply waiting for it to accidentally cross your path. You plan your day with the intention of being sensitive to the needs of others.

Accidental good acts: Each day when you drive your car you are surrounded by good acts. These are the drivers who are careful not to hit you. Because they protect themselves, They also look after you. Their act is good, but not intentional.

Concentrated good acts: Good acts are most concentrated where love is strongly and exclusively expressed. It seems that the nature of man and woman is to develop close, one-on-one relationships so that good acts have a massive, singular focus. It is a good atmosphere in which to begin family life and to saturate it with good acts.

Diluted good acts: Because certain human relationships are important for our stability, we concentrate our good acts in those connections. When we move outside of that boundary of meaningful, personal relationships our good acts lose their intensity. Our good acts turn into habitual good manners and polite words that embellish social decorum. Diluted good acts differ from concentrated good acts in that they are less permanent, less involved in commitment, and may be used as manipulations involving material gains.

Some Types of Needs

Healthy needs are essential requirements that help sustain our lives. These include food, water, clothing, shelter, and oxygen. Addictive needs involve a craving. These come in various categories and are very common—for example getting hooked on a drug, gambling, shopping, eating, or many others.

Any healthy need allows us to function optimally in both mind and body. Needs have different levels of intensity. In fact, we are often so preoccupied with our own needs that we can't see the everyday needs of others.

The need to be asked: In order for good to flow outward from a person you need to ask. The Salvation Army has its kettle, which asks for your good to flow. Toss in a buck, and your good has flowed, meaning it has gone from you, to the kettle, to a person in need. Similarly, anyone can easily get at least a little good to flow by asking.

"Ask and it shall be given unto you," said the Lord.

Surrounded by many shoppers at the grocery store, I was searching for an item. I decided to tap the resource standing conveniently just next to me. "Where do I find the Saran Wrap?" I asked my resource, a woman looking at the canned vegetables.

She stopped, put her hand to her chin, and replied, "Let me see—down by the pop and potato chips; one, two, three rows from the end."

"Thank you so much for your kindness," I replied. That pleasantly helpful person had tossed a coin into my kettle. It is like sprinkling God about in the grocery store. It is He who must certainly derive satisfaction from allowing His goodness to show.

The need to be noticed: Besides the need to be asked to help is the need to be noticed. For example, a man with a carton of cigarettes stood behind me in a checkout line. I noticed and asked, "You going to smoke all of them?"

"Yeah," he replied.

"Do you want to stop?"

"Been smoking since I was 15. I know I should."

"Good luck. Hope you make it."

"Thanks, I'll try."

Most people enjoy being noticed. Furthermore, it is an innocuous, simple act of giving value to someone. To notice him is to say he is worth noticing. It is like saying, "Hi there, I see that you exist." The cigarettes are but the go-betweens, the concrete items that are superficial to the person-to-person encounter. Thank goodness for the go-betweens. They are the keys that open the door to our hearts.

Need for a comfort zone: For good to flow freely it requires a need for an appropriate comfort zone.

It is wonderful to feel secure, especially about home. One morning when I was leaving home I overheard a neighbor say to her daughter, "Have a good day at school, honey, and I'm sorry I yelled at you."

"That is really neat," I thought. Stepping down from the parental pedestal and acknowledging a human frailty in front of your child is a powerful act of caring. An apology is a relaxant. It puts the mind at ease for both the offender and die offended. Coming from a parent it is especially important because it communicates the message, "All is well at home."

The need to believe in God: If you have a need to believe in God, then believe. If you don't believe, then there are abundant mind-changing influences in the world ready to help you. A belief in God is a stabilizing influence and a modifying or changing influence. It is an act whereby you open the door for God's goodness to pass through you into a needy world.

*   *   *

When Bill was 26 years old he had a conversion. He was a "bad boy" until then, drinking and womanizing. He heard some preacher talking here, another there; it was getting to him. His dormant conscience was stirring. Then Bill concluded, "I can die and go to Hell." Suddenly he was afraid. He called it "the fear of the l-ord." It made him change. Now the former "bad" Bill can recite quotes from the Bible just like Billy Graham. Today it is virtually impossible for him to give up his relationship with God.

I am the same way, but I never did have that conversion. God is in my soul, in every cell of my body. But Bill says my state of grace is less than his because I had no conversion. I wonder why am I wrong, and he is right. You let well enough alone if the need to believe in God is satisfied. There is no need to say, "My need is legitimate, but yours is incomplete." This is exactly the issue and reason, I contend, that started the crusades and holy wars. It is exactly the reasoning of religious intolerance and, consequently, bloodshed in the world today. Bill is demonstrating beautifully, though in a smaller way, an act of intolerance.

The mind can twist anything and make it look right. If you hurt your neighbor, just say it is God's wish and he or she should be granted martyrdom for it. That doesn't sound like the caring, "Love thy neighbor" kind of God I know. You can reference the name of God to anything. It is just an erroneous application of a word. If the result is not loving one another or being good to one another, helping, sharing, and being unified, it has nothing to do with God.

With belief, God fuses with your mind and soul. You can't shake it. You are Him. You live Him; you breathe Him. Your need for God is firmly placed. At this point you are not interested about a detail in the Bible that you missed. At this point you are not interested in the atheistic position that God is an illusion. You want compassion and understanding, mostly in terms of being left alone with your satisfied state of mind.

Let the person who believes believe. Tolerance means don't tamper with that fusing between a person and his God when his spiritual need has already been accommodated. If not, that person is fair game for persuasion by Bill or anybody else who is evangelizing. Otherwise, hands off, because you may be questioning or nitpicking at that very belief that sustains a person. It is serious business because you are not only attacking what he believes, but, because his belief has become him, you are attacking him.

Anticipating a Good Act

I will move about as I ordinarily do, through a maze of straight-aways and bends, turns and bumps, one day at a time. Each day there will be a time when the maze will reveal its needful secrets. Awaiting the need, I will take my talent, courage, and awareness, and, whether I stand in line at McDonald's or wait for a traffic signal to change, my mind will alertly anticipate the encountering someone's need. I will see weaker arms and lend my stronger arms. I will see someone lost and give direction. To one needing talk, I will listen closely. I will be servant-like and be alert to the crying out of the need. I will act as if I were doing it for someone I loved dearly.

Knowing that I cannot do alone what I have outlined for myself to do, I will ask for the help of a counselor to accompany me. My spiritual friend will give me courage to do what was needed and joy when I can taste the sprinkle of goodness that I give. In this life I will do all the good I can, remembering:

> *I can influence the future;*
> *I can improve on my past.*
> *I'll seek a Mission Moment,*
> *a good act that will last.*
> *With love I'll fill that moment,*
> *for it will pass away.*
> *The chance will be lost forever,*
> *if I do not care today.*

May I Tell You What You Like to Hear?

I went about my routine business today with one exception: I was telling more people than usual what I liked about them. A lady was sitting in a wheelchair. "Hello," I said, "are you able to walk?"

"A little," she replied.

"You're dress is so beautiful." She smiled, her husband smiled, and both said "Thank you."

I then went to the photography department to get pictures. "How in the world can you keep trim like that?" I remarked to a young woman standing near me. "What is your secret?"

She smiled and remarked proudly, "And I eat everything."

I went to get brakes checked on the car. I was able to say something nice to a mechanic who was lacking sleep. To an elderly man who kept working hard at his job I gave concern, and to a baker, who was worried about passing his test to be a Master Baker, I gave words of hope.

I realized I was telling people things they liked to hear, but none of them were asking for it. I did this to acknowledge a positive characteristic of each. It was saying, "Hi there; I acknowledge you are not only there, but you are there for me; I am not only here, but I am here for you." I think it's in the context of fellowship that I tell people what they like to hear, that they may think better of themselves.

II
The Mission Moment

In this life you can stand, sit, or lie down. 'There is one other thing you can do—move. You will pass this day but once. At its end you can look at yourself, asking, "What good act did I do?"

Not every good act is a mission, but every mission involves the pursuit of a good act. Upon wakening, you prayerfully resolve to find the courage, strength, and especially the alertness to assure that you do not miss the moment when your good act and another's need should meet.

With your birth you have been given the gift of space, carrying it around wherever you may go. Most likely the calling of a mission moment will occur in the surroundings of your space. Yet because of our human frailty you have the freedom to say, "Today I don't feel like it; I'm not m the mood; I won't do it."

Though a mission moment may be challenging, the need has a pulling effect on us. Requiring fulfillment, we are drawn to help. Like a magnet we are pulled, egged on by our compassion and the striving for a satisfaction, for a completion of the needy task.

Sometimes commitment reflects a giving mode that is not at the level of an unselfish move. We may, of course, abort at any nine. Our choice is always our choice. But with every new success the confidence in performing any mission moment increases.

It is difficult to know precisely when we have a "go" for a mission moment. In fact, we may be halfway through the good act before we realize that we are involved. To start off as an ordinary, kind-hearted person is a natural beginning. The mission moment evolves as one decides on a super- good, unconditional treatment where the common person is made to feel particularly special.

The quest for a mission moment can vary in intensity. To intuitively allow ourselves to be guided by the need requires faith, a realization that such a format gives direction and guidance to our lives.

The mission moment represents a decision to increase the dignity and worth of any person who is chosen. The objectives are:

> *1. To treat another as you would*
> *someone you love.*
> *2. To embellish the good act so that it is not a*
> *common nor ordinary transaction. It would*
> *have impact unlikely to be forgotten.*

To touch a soul is an appropriate description of the mission moment. When we touch a soul, we have created a sameness between persons. The giver of the good act and the receiver become alike in that they are in peaceful harmony.

When our goodness reaches a sublime level where every person feels like a family member who is loved, then we have the recipe for peace on earth.

* * *

My hitchhiker's name was Phil. All of his belongings were stuffed inside the two duffel bags he carried. A $600 check each month helped sustain him. Though some people are guided by the prospect of work in a community, Phil moved about the country guided primarily by rent values. Intermittently, Phil commented about the beauty of the scenery as we drove through the rolling hills of Wyoming. "Where you going?" he asked me.

"South Dakota. I turn on route 90," 1 replied.

Phil reached back for his bag on the rear seat and pulled out an atlas. Looking at it carefully he suggested, "You can let me off just before Buffalo because 90 turns about six miles before Buffalo." Phil put his atlas back and said. "I'm hungry. Haven't eaten anything since yesterday."

We were approaching Sheridan when I asked Phil, "Do you have any brothers?"

"One," he replied

"And what does he do?"

"He's a grammar-school teacher in Fresno."

"And your parents, do they live in Fresno too?"

"Yeah, but I don't know if they're alive anymore."

We looked carefully for the correct exit to take into Sheridan, intent on finding a Hardee's. In fact, Phil was so intent on making it a Hardee's stop that we had run out of exits. We were again in the wide-open country, heading toward Buffalo. Within half an hour we were at the route 90 junction.

"Let me off here," my exhausted passenger requested.

I was at a fork in the road. Then I decided Phil would be my family member. He would be my mission moment. "I'll drive you into Buffalo," I responded and kept going.

In Buffalo we began searching for a reasonable motel for Phil. We were also interested in knowing where bus tickets to Casper could be purchased. After searching around we were unable to purchase a bus ticket because there were no buses going directly to Casper. But we did find a motel for twenty-five dollars.

My friend decided that he wanted something to eat badly. We drove around looking for a hamburger place. Then he asked me, "Wanna share a pizza?"

Since I was driving, I brought us to a steak house instead. "I can't afford this," my friend said quietly as he looked at the fancy sign with trepidation. Receiving the menu, Phil ordered a waffle. It wasn't even listed.

"A steak for my friend," I told the waitress, "a New York Steak. And, as for me, I'll have soup and salad," I said.

"How come you're giving me the big piece of meat, and you're having soup and salad?" queried Phil.

"'Cause you deserve it."

After finishing his meal and placing the extra rolls and butter into a napkin, Phil acknowledged, in a most sincere manner, "This is the nicest meal I have ever had. Thank you for picking me up."

"Thank you for joining me in my space, Phil."

We returned to one of the less expensive motels that Phil had liked earlier. Twenty-four fifty was the cost of the room. My friend reached for a bag where he kept his money, but I was faster. I paid for the room and then said "good luck," to my friend. I shook his hand and grabbed his shoulder.

"Thank you," he said, with tears showing.

"Thank you for being on the road, Phil."

Phil wanted to say goodbye, but that was hard for him, so we just stood quietly and awkwardly looked at each other. Then Phil spoke, almost as if he never before uttered those words to anyone, "Drive carefully."

I backed the car out, and, as I turned on to the main street, there my friend stood, waving a last farewell. That was a moment of great essence, of strangers who met on the highway and touched souls. We had known each other forever.

* * *

Three Cubans came to be with us because we had asked for them—Maria, the mother, Soledad, her pregnant daughter, and Uberto, her daughter's husband. Ours was the only family in South Dakota who sponsored a Cuban refugee family. They spoke Spanish and no English. We spoke English and no Spanish. They were poor. They arrived by plane from Fort Chaffee practically barefoot and without belongings. The presence of the Cubans in our small community exposed prejudice. They were resented because they received food stamps to help sustain them.

Domestic problems became evident quickly among the trio. The mother, sixty-nine, insisted on being first in her daughter's life, while Uberto insisted that the mother-in-law should not interfere in his marriage. In our home the three Cubans frequently fought with each other. We acquired the help of two Spanish-speaking interpreters and periodically held counseling meetings to resolve family conflicts.

They lived with us in our home for forty-one days. On the forty-first day they decided to go and "live with their kind" in Miami They were able to save up money while they had worked at a local butcher shop, and they wanted to start a new life in Miami.

On leaving by bus from Sioux Falls, they carried two suitcases of clothing. Their health needs had been cared for (all had been anemic), and they gave the appearance, at least, of some respectability.

The Cubans were given to us completely exposed, and we gave them a sense of dignity. Nobody paid us for what we did. We provided medical services, bought clothes and shoes, arranged visits to the hair salon, arranged for food stamps and Social Security benefits for the mother, and gave them what useful belongings we had to offer, including suitcases, for the trip to Miami. Our contribution was a mission moment, forty-one days long. Their success was a home in Miami where Uberto studied auto mechanics and eventually succeeded in that profession, despite having a deformed left arm. When we last heard from them they had two beautiful daughters and they were living comfortably in Miami.

* * *

I was sitting in an apartment, 13,000 miles from home, looking out the window and musing about the long trip. We departed from Detroit sixteen hours ago. It was an agonizing experience because I had an unrelenting toothache. Even if I survived the nine-day vacation that was planned, the return trip would not be pleasant. I needed someone to

help
me. "Help, help, help," I asked quietly, prayerfully.

The very next day, early in the morning, I sat in the same chair, looking at the skyscrapers as they rose high above the streets below.

The slap of rubber came from my left as latex gloves were adjusted to fit a petite hand. An angel, Rolyn, was there, asking me to "open up." Then she looked into my mouth, prodding the affected tooth gently with a long, silver instrument. It was infected and would require ampicillin three times a day for seven days. Rodney, her boyfriend and my nephew, brought the medicine within minutes. Her dentistry skills and her gentle touch reassured me completely. Tomorrow I would come to Rolyn's clinic.

The office was clean and restful. As she talked, intending to make me feel comfortable, Rolyn kept calling me 'Uncle." Apparently she had adopted me through her relationship with my nephew.

The x-ray showed a very deep cavity. The tooth would have to be removed. Rolyn would prepare, clean, and medicate it so that my journey home would be comfortable. There was no transaction for the service. It came free. The gush of goodness from Rolyn had overwhelmed me. I was the unexpected mission moment of another, and I was bathed in the wonder of it. Her generous, good act and my need met almost as if designed by heaven itself.

The experience gave me an uplifting feeling as if I were being treated with considerable dignity and worth. In a foreign land, I felt the love of family deeply.

III
Good Acts in Action

When Nobody Is Looking

Two children were playing, a boy and a girl. The boy, about eight, was trying to spin his sister around. She refused to cooperate, making the boy more determined to give her a twirl. Then he raised his right arm, about to strike her. At that very moment he caught a glimpse of a pair of eyes looking directly at him, mine. Quickly, he dropped that threatening arm. Now, when he played, he looked up to see if those same two eyes were still watching.

The boy knew the difference between good and not good, yet he didn't refrain from slapping his sister on his own. He thought that, if no one was looking, he could get away with it.

I happened to come across a toilet that ran continuously. I listened to it and thought, "A lot of water is being wasted here." But the toilet wasn't mine and I was in a hurry—and I would mess up my clothes. There was nobody else there. Nobody would know if I fixed it or didn't fix it. "Let the owner get a plumber; interfering only gets you into trouble," I reasoned. "Why not walk out like every one before me did and let that water keep running until somebody's well went dry." But I shouldn't let that happen. I was in conflict. I tried to imagine that this property was my own, trying to nudge myself in a positive direction. Yet, it didn't matter what I imagined, I would be doing something good for nothing because nobody would see me do it.

I did the good act finally. I lifted the top of the water container and looked in. After removing one, two, three, four, five empty coke cans the water stopped running. Suddenly I had become the invisible being, an unknown guardian angel battling my own distractions and excuses. Most of all, I did it because someone was there with me.

The little boy was stopped from striking his sister because my eyes were looking at him. I was stopped from walking away because someone was also watching me. For me it was my conscience, a pair of eyes that belonged to many people: my mom, dad, teachers, priest, neighbors, and friends—all contributing to my character. They taught me to obey, to say "yes" even though nobody else was around. Without them I may very well have said "no" and dropped in another coke can.

I fixed the toilet, and, to this day, I don't know who I did it for. It would not be too embarrassing if I just said I did it for God. If you do not know for whom you do a good act, you can always turn to God and say, "Here, this one is for You."

A Good Act Is as Long as a Sentence

How wonderful it is to take care of ourselves and our own needs. Receive a smile, hear a cheerful "good morning," enjoy a friendly dog, let someone hold the door for you, let someone bring you the newspaper, stand up and give you his or her seat, bring you coffee, or give you a hug. We accommodate ourselves and allow others to be good to us.

Enjoy being first because, in order to give goodness, we must first know the feel of it and want to share it.

Need is a total functioning. It is both take and give, in that order. Receive a good act for yourself, learn from it, and bask in its wonder. Then carry it and cross-pollinate like the bee; share it, and fulfill the needs of others. It is perhaps no surprise that there are some things we can do to meet a need that are as inexpensive as a breath of air and more valuable than the treasures of King Midas.

A Good Act Gives Hope

Just before Christmas Day I met Albert. He was chipper for a man of eighty-one. Though his knee was swollen he walked in his garden because it would strengthen his failing heart. He explained how wonderful it feels to be alive despite the fact that he had prostate and colon cancer and had had most of his bowels removed. His cardiologist said he had three months to live.

Albert did not need a new hat, a watch, or a ton of pure gold for Christmas. He needed life. "You will live for ten more years, and I will come to celebrate your ninety-first birthday," I told him confidently.

"I wish my cardiologist was saying what you just said," he replied.

"Better than that," I responded irreverently, "I am right."

That wrinkled face brightened. The smile, the dancing eyes, the sense of gratitude and hope had refreshed that flagging spirit. Revitalized, he turned to his rich past and gave me a personal invitation to hear him play several "oldies" tunes on his guitar.

An Act of Caring

You can use a word or phrase that ordinarily belongs to a close relationship and apply it to a stranger.

* * *

I had anxious moments in Pittsburgh because this was the third plane I was assigned, and each had delays due to bad weather. I hurried to the gate. Soon I was facing a young girl at the ticket counter. She was coughing.

"I'm sorry you're not feeling well," I remarked.

"How did you know?" she asked.

"Sounds like you need cough medicine."

"That's right," she agreed.

"You must take care of yourself. I care about you."

"But you just met me," the girl replied with surprise. "How can you care about me?"

"Because you remind me of my daughter whom I love very much."

I took my ticket and sat down. My seat was number 16D. Seconds later, I felt a tapping on my shoulder. It was the same girl. On my ticket she wrote, "Upgrade, first class, 6D."

My words, "I care for you" implied intimacy. When I associated her with my own daughter our relationship developed warmth. Now she was feeling as if I meant what I said and believing she was embraced by a family's love.

Quite generally, we do separate the good we say at home from the good we say away from home. However, try not to separate it, but —

Wherever you trod,
wherever in life you roam,
Bring along the word,
"I care for you."
And make some
stranger feel at home.

The Good Act and Loneliness

Michael, my grandson, and I were sitting in a restaurant. I overheard an elderly woman asking someone for a number. I casually turned to the woman and asked, "How are you?"

"I'm mad, mad, mad. I didn't get my food yet."

I quickly learned her name, Myrtle, and that she was selling her home and moving to Missouri, that she had two children and five grandchildren, that she had lost her husband seven years ago, and that they were married forty-four years. Poor thing, she needed someone to talk to.

"It's tough being alone," she said, with a sigh. I listened attentively to her reminiscing about her past. Just as the waitress brought her food, Myrtle made a move to change positions. She came closer. My attention was riveted on her. I could not help but to think that, for that moment, she was more important than my food. I positioned myself halfway into the aisle to accentuate my interest in her. Michael had no idea what Grandpa was doing. "Let's go, Grandpa," was all he could say. But I was not about to go anywhere as long as the little old lady had something to say. As our conversation was creeping to an end I asked, "Can I give you a hug?"

She stood up and flung her arms around me. Myrtle approached Michael for a hug also, but he moved away, a frightened bunny.

Remember to give a hug to some lonely person every day.

Soothing a Restless Soul

I had a telemarketer call recently who wanted to give me something free: 4 subscriptions to 4 magazines, all free, "If you change your phone service."

"That isn't 'free,'" I responded, "not if you are saying, 'if.' In our town 'free' means there are no strings attached."

He called the word free a business word and that should make it acceptable to everyone. At that point our conversation seemed to have ended, but he wasn't hanging up. He wanted to talk more about something.

I quickly discovered that he was the son of a preacher, and that he was raised by a grandfather who also was a preacher. The telemarketer's name was Joshua. "You churchgoing?" I asked.

Surprisingly he said, "No, I'm not."

"I would expect you to be preacher number three," I told him. Joshua changed the subject abruptly. He started talking about evolution. I collected my thoughts and said, "Everything you give as proof of God's non-existence can also be construed as. God's plan."

We talked and talked for about a half hour. Joshua was troubled by the many gods who are worshipped. "Which is the right one?" he wanted to know. lie called himself an agnostic because he wanted to make up his own mind.

I wasn't going to tell him where to worship or how. I told him that I sensed a struggle inside of him.

"I don't want you to have those violent struggles between believing and not believing," I told him. "I want you to be at peace. Let your mind dwell on knowing that God is good."

Joshua's voice was calmer. I sensed meekness, relaxation, and humility. He was finding an inner peace in the goodness of God.

A Good Act in New Orleans

Cordelia, a waitress named after a character in Shakespeare's King hear, came over to our table. Where is your usual?" she asked me. Seeing I didn't have it, she promptly brought the usual for me. It arrived in a glass.

"Have you been here before?" Justina, a colleague, asked, "How come you get special treatment?"

The only thing I had done was tell Cordelia that she was a good person. I had observed her and was impressed by her efficient manner and courtesy. By acknowledging and celebrating her goodness, it seemed I had helped Cordelia become proud of herself, and she wanted to be more attentive and caring.

My entire contact with the waitress at the Hilton was about four minutes long. Yet we were instantly bonded by the power of goodness as if we were friends forever. Leaving the Hilton in New Orleans, I reached into my bag where I had a reserve of goodness messages that I carry just for such occasions. "This is for you," I said to that wonderful waitress.

That good in you, from your heart it does flow; For eternity it will glow, And all creation, from your birth, Shall know with God you've walked the earth.

My last recollection of Cordelia was seeing her wiping a tear, and proudly smiling and passing the message around to her co-workers.

When someone does a good job it is the person's goodness that shows. Therefore, you may tell him or her, "You are a good person." It is deeper, more meaningful than the more common, "Good job." Try it. See if you notice a difference.

* * *

Perhaps you realize that liking a person has more conditions than you've thought about. Self-centered people might be off your list; people who talk too much may not be likable; even bald-headed people who are bow-legged may be crossed off. Eventually you may settle for family members who are likable, but you are not even sure about one or two of those. All else failing, you discover that a cat or a canary is about right, but not both together.

The Good Act of Listening

In Seattle there is a structure called the Space Needle. An elevator takes you up about 200 feet, and you arrive at a circular platform on top from which you can see miles around. I visited and brought a camera along. Melvin, an African-American whom I had never met before, saw my camera and asked, "What kind is it?" Noticing that I was reasonably receptive, Melvin decided to talk to mc. I listened as best as I could as the circular top of the needle turned slowly around until the sky turned a misty gray.

Melvin told me many things about himself, from his childhood in Oklahoma to his success as a parent of eight children in Los Angeles. Melvin sounded like a salesman. He wanted to feel good about himself and needed to be reassured. I shook Melvin's hand, and told him how impressed I was with his achievements and how pleased I was to have met him. Melvin gave me personal information, and I gave him my approval. He wasn't interested in my camera at all. He was interested in knowing that he was a good person, so I told him that he was. He just needed to hear it from someone.

Listening to a one-sided conversation is uncomfortable to most, but that is my favorite kind because of the opportunity to learn about others.

Those who suffer loneliness require your patience, a listening ear, support, and expressions of approval.

"Don't Go!"

I do not live in the West Central neighborhood in Spokane, Washington, but I am watching out for the children there. I go there to give a neighborly hand to struggling parents who are trying to make ends meet. I help their children make correct choices in life so they can grow up to be decent, happy adults.

I volunteer at the West Central Community Center during the school year. I get there at about 3:00 p.m., waiting for forty to fifty elementary school children to come in, make noise, and run around the gymnasium. Eventually they settle down and interact with friends, play games, jump rope, or bounce a ball. Their age ranges from five to eleven. After about an hour, parents come from work to pick up their children.

Meanwhile I try to impart to the children values for life. I use what resources are available. For example, tossing a ball to a child you have never met before and having him throw it back to you can start an instant relationship. You can cause laughter, you can teach and learn, challenge, bring out the best in good sportsmanship, give attention, have fun, exercise, socialize, increase self-confidence, compete to win, and be creative. A child who is shy or has nobody to play with always gets a toss of a ball and an invitation to play. I also like the rebel type, the kid who says no to everything. I might put him in charge of a ball-tossing contest, praise him for his great job, and watch him shine.

I'd like to think that my contribution to the children of West Central will have a life-long impact on them. Such qualities as responsibility, forgiveness, respect, and patience are objectives for a better life. The Activities Director and I would observe improvements in the children and single them out for special recognition.

I had learned that children are usually willing to let you be a part of their lives. If a child likes you and trusts you, it is easier for her to listen to you. If you can show her a right way, she will use that way. It can stick with her a whole lifetime.

An adult shows appreciation by saying, "Thank you!" a child by saying, "Don't go!"

IV
Manifestations of Sacrifice

The Random Acts of Kindness Organization requested that people write letters describing an act of kindness. Ninety letters were read. I read each kindness story and placed each into one of three categories: Take, Observe, and Give. Of the ninety letters, forty-two described an act of kindness where they were the recipient or taker; thirty-two described an act of kindness where they were the observer of a kind act occurring between others. Sixteen of the ninety reported a random act of kindness describing themselves as giving kindness to others.

Evaluating the three groups briefly, I chose to be a taker. I would prefer to have a kindness done to me. The extent of the inconvenience that occurred in the kindness acts might represent a mild sacrifice.

Consider this next incident. The driver went 20 miles further to accommodate Harry, a hitchhiker. "Thanks," he told the driver. "People are not usually kind anymore." I'd like to be Harry, the recipient of the good act. That was a wonderful service, being driven to my destination, bolstering my self-worth free of charge. As for the sacrifice experienced by the driver, it was only at about a moderate level.

Sacrifice Has Different Objectives

It was hard to think that every person I gave a bag of groceries to was dying of AIDS. It made me so sad. Yes, we do clean toilets. This is cool because it teaches us cooperation skills and how to have a servant's heart. I have been able to save money from working during the summers, and now I am going to the Philippines. I have joined YWAM, Youth With A Mission.

These words are contained in a letter from Alana. I have known her since she was ten. She is clearly moving her space so that another's needs are more accessible to her good acts. The light of her goodness shines through with obedience to a higher power.

* * *

The snows came to her town, and sixteen-year-old Alice was given a school project on character development. She chose to shovel the snow from her neighbors' walks, the rule was that she could not accept any money. Certainly, it was a good act with sacrifice.

To compare Alana and Alice it is necessary to look at the source. With Alana the motivation comes from within. Stimulated by the awareness of an externally perceived need, Alana responds with an inner compassion. Alice needed an assignment to prompt her sacrificial good act. Alana is accountable to a higher power; Alice is accountable to a teacher requiring an assignment. One is faith-driven and will, therefore, be continuous; the other is grade-driven and, therefore, should be expected to cease when the grade is achieved.

V
Reciprocating God's Goodness

God decided to give you a gift, you. You were a gift to you. Once you were created God followed you around. He wanted to appreciate His creation. He gave you special recognition, a helping hand in rough places, and he called it "good." And I think He said, "Go and do likewise." You have been given yourself, priceless and worthy of recognition.

Volunteers are exceptional persons because they relish performing good acts. Many are life-long, professional good-act givers. In one local hospital there are 500 volunteers, and more are asking for the opportunity to join. They get awards in the form of pins; they get a pink outfit and a party once a year, and they devote over 17,000 hours of good-act giving a month. They do it out of a desire to care and share the outpouring of their own goodness.

One seventy-year-old, a new volunteer, pointing to his protruding dome-shaped belly, said, "I am requesting lots of walking." Interaction with others, maintaining schedules, and behaving with purpose keeps the mind sharp and the spirit gratified. Longevity is the reward. You live longer, being more satisfied with a life that has meaning.

Jack the grocer closes his business each Wednesday afternoon and visits the elderly at a local nursing home. He has followed this routine undetected for years. Now Jack is noticed by a reporter. To reinforce his humble image he tells the reporter what he is doing amounts to "nothing." Nevertheless, the report of Good-Act-Jack is spread. They said he played bingo for one who was sick and helped her move her swollen hand. He wiped her nose and brushed her clothes, then said, "Thank you" for her being there. Then he took her swollen hand to his cheek and shed a tear.

He is celebrated in the newspaper and, instead of remaining unobtrusively humble, he becomes unexpectedly popular. He has become identified by many as the Very Good Person who visits the elderly. Soon those who have senior relatives in the nursing home are asking Jack to visit them. Thus the flow of God's goodness, through Jack the grocer, increases so that more can feel the touch of His love.

Go forth in life, so profuse,
And see from God what you can use.
Let it mean to some person
The joy of heart, the warmth of sun.
Though hills and valleys fall away
The good you give will ever stay.

If I Am Good to You, Will You Be Good to Me?

Four-year-old Emily is your grandchild. You go into the house. Emily looks down, bends over, and unties your shoelaces. "I know where shoes go," she says confidently, removing both shoes and placing them in a closet. Emily wants you to stay.

You sit down on the couch. "My feet are cold," you say.

"I can do it," Emily responds enthusiastically, bringing a blanket and covering your feet. She is responding to your need; she is taking care of you. "What would you like to drink, Gampa?"

'Tea, black tea."

"And what kind of cookie?"

"Oreo, black."

Emily carries the message to mother; "Gampa wants tea, black, and an Oreo Cookie, black." She can't fulfill the request alone, but she knows who can.

Emily is saying, "Look how important you are to me, Gampa."

From you, Emily gets a hug, a kiss, a story, a chance to sit on your ankle and get an up-and-down ride, and a clap when she draws something. Together you walk in the garden, sit, and watch the birds.

You are saying, "Look how important you are to me, Emily." One's entire life's ambition may rest with one single, yet precious need, to feel important to someone.

The 'Thank You"

In our family gatherings we typically pray by expressing a number of "thank yous" at mealtime. Over Thanksgiving the "thank yous" given are usually more expressive. We hear "thank You Lord" incessantly from those who preach on television. I know my Grandchildren, when they forget to say "thank you" are promptly reminded. Are we a "thank you" oriented society? Maybe it is because we have so much to be thankful for. How special it is to receive from God his goodness and to thank him for it.

I find it much easier to give a thank you than receive one. Receiving a thank you is hardly ever mentioned. In prayers, for example, we can say, "Thank you Lord for my good acts because today I received thirteen 'thank yous.'"

When God saw that Adam was alone, He created for him a companion. God acted on the basis of Adam's need. Adam most certainly responded to this magnificent act with a big "thank you."

Being God-like requires helping someone in need, just as God helped Adam. When you help someone, you open the door for a "thank you." That is the same kind of "Thank you" that God hears in prayers that rise up to heaven. That is the best proof of God within us, reaching out to others and working wonders.

* * *

Out of a bunch of toys I asked my 6-year-old grandson to choose the very best toy to give to a boy who had none. He chose an old, cracked helmet. It looked like it was run over by a truck. It wasn't his best toy; it was his worst. What my grandchild is expecting is the best for himself; what he gives is the worst for others.

I decided to go to his first grade class with nine lollipops, and I gave my grandson one. With permission from the teacher, we were going to play a "thank you" game. "Watch how many 'thank yous' I can get," I told my grandson, turning to several children sitting in a row. As quickly as I gave a lollipop I heard a "thank you." Now it was my grandson's turn. He gave away his lollipop grudgingly. When he heard the "thank you" coming right back he sort of smiled.

So, if we are teaching our children to say "thank you" for the good done to them, we should encourage them to focus on the importance of the "thank yous" they receive for the good they've done to others.

It is never too early for the child to know how it feels to be God-like.

VI
The Wonder of Obedience

The armed services are in the business of making people listen. If you can't take an order, you're out. In society if you can't listen and follow the law, you face certain consequences. In school if you can't listen to the teacher and follow the rules, you fail.

Furthermore, radio, TV, the newspaper, the mail, and the Internet come at you like a horde of buffalo with an onslaught of "listen to me" messages.

Authentic quotations of frustrated parents include, "She knows it all and will not listen," or "I have tried to talk to him, but he will not listen." Many have uttered, in desperation, "Why can't somebody ever listen to me for a change?"

If you live in that state of unfulfilled need, craving to have someone do what you ask them, have I got good news for you. I found a child who listens.

"Maddie," I said, "will you please put your shoes in your bedroom?" Just one time I spoke, and Maddie went off happily with her shoes and carried them to her bedroom. On the way she also picked up her socks. Instinctively, Maddie knows what is right. She anticipates what you would like her to do, and she does it before you even ask, reducing the strain on your vocal chords. She will pour her own cereal and eat her creamed corn and boiled carrots. She will drink her milk, and there is no fuss whatsoever because that's what you wanted her to do in the first place. Maddie has faith in you and trusts you that you will be faithful to her needs and keep her secure.

The act of listening and obeying can have a profound impact on the course of history. Jesus, listening to His Father, said, "Not Mine, but Your will be done." It would have been a significantly different story if He had responded, "No, I don't have to."

When the angel came to Mary with the good news that she was chosen to bear the Christ Child, it would have been a different story if she had said, "I don't think so."

It is from that faith that a little child has in us that we understand our obedience to God.

Indeed, a little child obeys in pure faith, opens our eyes, and shows us the way of the Lord.

VII
The Good That Love Brings

The Family, a Love Factory

A significant objective in family life is to establish an environment for children to receive good acts and to be prepared to perform good acts for others. The family is the training ground, the love factory that produces goodness-giving children, a condition that will assist them in finding happiness in the world.

Imagine in one hand I hold water; in the other hand I hold dirt. Suppose I bring both together and make a stream. A stream flows, and it weaves and does more. Between the water and the dirt there is cooperation, a giving in. And so the stream of water achieves its purpose: it weaves down to the sea. Two separate things are meant to come together and make one very good thing. The same applies to the family, which consists of two parents. The coming together of man and woman in the family setting is like the dirt and water coming together. Coming together they raise one good, the child, who has a totality of ingredients, both of mother and of father.

There is love in good acts. If a child is deprived in the family, the lifelong journey of searching for that love can result. Those who speak of a breakdown in the family are imprecise. A family must have a healthy structure before it can break down. Unhealthy or dysfunctional families maintain the behavior similar to street conduct, manifesting a paucity of good acts. If a child does not differentiate behavior between home and street conduct it is easy to flow from one lifestyle to another. Because the home is no different from any other place, running away from it is easier. In a home where good acts are practiced and family members are treated specially, runaways are much less likely. The contrast with life on the streets is so obvious that there is no thought of fleeing into certain stress and discomfort.

Belonging to Someone

Belonging is extremely important because it is a condition that sets firm a foundation in a relationship. From the spirit of belonging comes a security that is supportive of a richer development of two persons.

"Do you love me? Am I special to you?" one may ask of the other.

"Yes, yes, yes, a thousand time, yes," is your confirming answer, "I belong to you."

He was tall and slender, about twenty-two. In forty- degree weather he wore just a vest with long, bare arms protruding. He had a bald head and a three-inch goatee. From the side he looked like a goat.

I took hold of his arm as he stood by my table intently reading my romance cards which were on display at the First Baptist Craft Show. "Are you a romantic?" I asked.

He spoke affirmatively, though shyly, giving me the impression that he was an unassuming tough dude right out of the bad side of town. He wore three kinds of jewelry, a thin gold ring on his left ear, a dagger on his right car, and a thin silver orb stuck through a nostril.

At that moment a witch appeared. She was a foot shorter than the goat with a large, old-fashioned black hat that had a brim extending a foot from her face, giving the impression that she was in perpetual darkness. Her body was draped in a Batman-type covering which dragged along the floor. 'You have a fine friend," I told her. The compliment caused her to grab his arm possessively.

Fondly she looked up at his slightly blushed and grimacing face and said with pride, "I know." It was enough. There was love there; I saw the sparks. To reinforce the belonging, the Goat reached across the table and chose Love Forever.

He passed the card to the witch, who read:

I give you my commitment,
we will never, never part;
Til death do us part
is far too soon for me;
Our love needs forever
in that land beyond the sea.
Our souls will blend among the stars
forever and a day
In lovely rose filled gardens
beyond the Milky Way.
This is my prayer, my darling
though the Lord only knows,
That we love where the stars are
and go where heaven goes.

"Secrets of a Romantic Man "
Greeting card series by Phil Stack

The witch held the card to her heart and looked lovingly into the goat's eyes. It was a good-act moment for hugging—the two people, a goat and a witch, belonged to one another.

The Good in Being a Romantic Man

This is how I am regarded by some people I know at hating time:

Mother: "I hate the way Dad wears his Sunday clothes to play with the dogs."

Greg: "I hate the way Dad puts five gallons in the car at a time and then runs out of gas."

Larry: "Do you ever look at Dad's eyeballs; how they shift from side to side—like he's trying to find a problem?"

Phil: "Dad is starting to walk bow-legged."

Lucy: "And I hear him burp at the table."

It is hard to practice my Romantic Man ways there. The key is in having found a true love—

I looked for true loves
o'er mountains and plains;
I looked 'neath the willows
that weep in the lanes.
In the heat of the sands;
in the silence of snow;
I looked 'til I found
where all true loves grow ...
From the best of two worlds
came two wonderful loves:
The love of my Lord

and the Love of my Life.

I just had a forty-four-year anniversary. I can say from good experience that you have to pull together to make it work; you place the relationship always first. If it is fraying, you mend it You live relentlessly in the courtship spirit Words of endearment keep you feeling youthful. You grow old together—you mellow, you blend into one, and, like solid steel, nothing can break you.

I am not a Valentino or a suave, handsome movie star—but let me tell you the secret of a romantic man. First, you grow her sense of /. Make it your specialty. She'll not get weary hearing how great she looks and how wonderful she is. Then hold her close, and see her aglow as your sweet words continue to make her grow. Then give a "God bless you" to her sneeze, a "thank you" for a kindness, and a warm and gentle "please." Touch her with tender warmth, build her self-esteem, fill her heart with words of love, then sit with her and dream.

And if she cares to ask your help, give it happily. Don't let forty-four years change your, "Just for you, my dear," "Happy to do it, darling," "Thank you for asking, my sweet." That courtship mood is always neat.

Your Soul-Mate

A couple of days ago I spoke to two divorced women. Each believed in a soul-mate, someone out there who is a perfect match. So why didn't they choose that one? They both thought they had, but their husbands changed.

Ninety-four percent of the unmarried in their twenties want a soul-mate for a spouse, and eighty-eight percent think there was a special person just waiting for them. Let's look at the criteria by which they chose that special person.

Of course, the choice must be uncontaminated. You cannot have perky hormones making the decision, or pick someone based on a defiant "I'll show Mother" attitude, or choose the one who has failed three previous soul-mate trials.

Furthermore, many soul-mate seekers are seeking maximum likeness for getting-along power. If that is a criterion for soul-mate selection, welcome to divorce court. Too much likeness can be the worst condition between two people. It is the differences that strengthen a marriage—too much likeness can eventually make life boring. Marriage is sustained by the challenge and excitement of differences.

In religious circles, soul—meaning spirit—is a revered concept. Your soul lives after you die. Your soul is the essence of your being. A person who is not seeking a soul-mate may find one evolving before his very eyes.

Suppose the soul-mate becomes a part of your life not in the beginning, but after a period of evolution, later on in a marriage. When all the fanfare and all the searching is done, she still finds you attractive, even when your appeal is long gone.

She gives beyond the limits of life, and loves you where the stars are, and eventually together you will go where heaven goes.

There are no instantaneous soul-mates. Soul-mates are not found. That is a fantasy. Soul-mates evolve in an atmosphere of tremendous reciprocation of love and goodness-giving.

Deep Love

When youngsters play baseball, they are often deluged with words of goodness from parents, even if their play is not superlative. Allowing a perfect pitch go by is a "good eye." Striking out is a "good try." Even losing a game is a "good show." As in baseball, working together to achieve a common goal applies in marriage where happiness is a desired objective.

As parents flaunt goodness as a positive incentive to a player, a marriage partner expresses a bias in favor of a loved one to help generate a happy relationship.

Exaggerated love incantations go along with the purposeful sharing of material wealth. Relinquishing property that it can belong to two helps solidify marital unity. Prior to a marriage you may feel that the other does not qualify to receive certain wealth. Therefore both sign a prenuptial agreement. It means you will not share your possessions with your darling spouse when the marriage ends. It anticipates a breakup that, in baseball terms, is like the parents telling their children they can expect to lose before the game begins.

To tamper with the oneness of a marriage is to interfere with its nobler objectives. But love can conquer that insensitive prenuptial mindset if the love bug bites hard enough.

With love you give value; with deep love you give great value. The more value you give your spouse, the more everything of yours becomes hers, and everything of hers becomes yours. She feels queen-like. Then yours is the privilege to enjoy riches that no amount of material wealth can purchase.

A Sudden Calling to Provide Family Love

My older sister, who is eighty-one, was placed in a nursing home recently. Then her only son died suddenly. The day of the funeral was approaching, and she had not been told. She constantly asked, "Where is Eddie; he's not coming to see me."

On the very day of the funeral she was told that Eddie died. She had her hair done, and she donned her gaudy party dress. In the church she was all smiling and bubbly, meeting and greeting the many neighbors and friends who arrived. Viewing the body, she said, "That's not Eddie; he is wearing no glasses." Then she walked away.

My sister refused to accept the reality of her tragedy that left her essentially bereft of a family. But she went further. She refused to accept the memory of the home she had lived in and insisted that her home was elsewhere. She rejected her married name and answered only to her maiden name. She wanted to erase from her mind her whole history of married life, so painful was the thought of facing her loss.

Here a mind is struggling to cope with life, though handicapped by Alzheimer's disease.

I have assured myself that not one week will go by for the rest of her life that my sister will not have visitations by friends or relatives. Her daughter will bring her home on weekend visits, her sister will drive her about town and show her die scenery, and all my children and grandchildren will send flowers, cards, and candy. We are a force of love to dispel the loneliness that her heart must feel for her loss. God created her for us to care for, and all of us to take care of each other as well.

There are many dozens more in the same facility with my sister who are abandoned. For them, no one comes; no one writes. Their agony, despair, and sense of hopelessness must be unbearable.

The Inspiring Goodness of a Father

I am a father of six children. I was a Mr. Mom before the role became fashionable. Bonding occurred early. I fed, changed diapers, and bathed the children. Putting them to sleep, I rocked them in my arms and sang. When they were a little older, I knelt and prayed at bedtime (we always blessed everybody in the whole wide world). I told a bedtime story and tucked them in with a good night kiss.

Later on I followed my children around and clapped for them. Football was big; so was track and baseball. The guy who watched excitedly at the sidelines was I. I attended faithfully every teacher's conference, sometimes being the only dad there. They understood how I felt. I knew they were smart because the teachers said so. "It doesn't matter how smart you are," I told them, "if you are not also good."

The role of a father is awesome. There is one indispensable gift a father gives his children that influences their character and future life profoundly: loving their mom, showing them how a man should treat a woman with care, respect, and romantic attentiveness. Of course, I knew what I was doing. I was preparing them for a significant part of their lives—marriage.

My wife and I were one item. We were one from the beginning. Pulling together, we gave the feeling that home was a secure place. With that dependable base the children could grow to their fullest potential.

I have five sons. I am most proud of the fact that they show respect and love to their wives. There are no divorces, and none are expected. Treating a wife with respect, dignity, and romanticism is an asset for a longer marriage.

A Mothers Love Requires No Toy

My mom had one attribute that stood out—though she could barely speak English, she could sense a need practically before it occurred. She knew how to be concerned, how to give comfort.

As you grow older you hope such finer, beautiful qualities of a parent rub off on you—and they do, for it was inescapable to carry into the wide world a measure of my mom's goodness.

Though I never received a single toy on any occasion, I always felt important in my family. We had practically nothing, yet I never had tantrums over it, and I never thought of running away because I was an unfulfilled child. My mom never said, "I want you to behave" or "I want you to be a good boy." She said instead, "God wants you to be good." That was my mom's way of teaching mc to have God as part of my life—and she taught me my evening prayers.

I was born in the Depression years where many people had nothing, but I was the luckiest kid alive because it felt great to be helping my family in hard times. I knew that God would think that a good child should do that. I had no presents, no television or computer. But I had a gift that would make a grown-up cry—I had a mom who loved me.

Show a Child the Good to Do

If you are irritated you yell, "I'm not feeling good," in hopes that the family turns quiet, and the kids slink into a cooperative mode. Your anti-irritant strategy is to say, "Stop it right now," "You're not supposed to," or "No, you'd better not."

If that doesn't work, you use the "get lost" approach. "Go outside and play," "Go to your room and stay there," or "Get out of my sight."

Unfortunately, if "get lost" doesn't work and "stop it" is repeated over and over until you are hoarse, then your irritability has become plainly worse. Of course, there is at least one child in the house at fault. He will pick up any bit of learning and carry it off to school. Being a kid who knows how to irritate, he is just what the new kindergarten teacher needs.

A "no" tells you what not to do. You don't learn from that. If you must use a no, also add a yes. For example, "No, not like that, but (yes) I will show you how." Also, "No, don't do that. This (yes) is how you hold the cat," or "No TV for an hour, but (yes) for 30 minutes."

"Yes" is a positive. It spells direction, and giving direction is a kind of caring. When you care, you teach. When you care, you set limits. So take your choice—yell "no!" until you've lost your voice, or show a child the good to do.

The Goodness Power of Children

My nemesis was a pipe first, then cigars. Some people pay their bills once a month; I paid my smoking dues with a monthly flare up of bronchitis. I could stop smoking briefly, a day or two at a time, but my willpower just fizzled out. It seemed there was nothing in the world that could give me the incentive to take better care of myself. My wife and I decided to have some semblance of order in the house. Six kids needed some sort of organizational pattern, so we decided to have a family government. Chores would be assigned for the week. Each would receive an envelope with a name and money amount written on it, just like some companies paid their workers. It was time to read the minutes by the secretary of that motley crew. Because Larry was assertive, he intruded on the proceedings of the meeting. He held a pitcher of water in one hand and, in the other, my newly-bought Swisher Sweets.

"Oh, no," I gasped, as he squeezed them until a filthy mush oozed out from between his fingers. Then he dunked them into the clear water until the liquid turned dark brown. Naturally, I stood up, protesting vigorously. A vote was being taken. My son announced, "Everybody who votes that Dad should stop smoking, raise your hand."

From that moment I never smoked again. I obeyed my children because they acted as if I was important to them. They gave me a gift, the gift of being good to myself.

VIII
Obstacles to the Flow of God's Goodness

Fear

A teacher was illustrating to a group of children how to act if approached by a stranger. They yelled and screamed, "No, no, no!" and they all ran away. But that every child who yells "No, no, no!" to a stranger today may be that very stranger seeking help tomorrow.

Here I am, out of gas. I need someone's good act to meet my need. I'm stranded off a busy highway between Des Moines and Indianapolis at midday. My hood is up, my white hanky is attached to my antenna, and I am pacing. Hundreds of vehicles are passing but a few feet away. Nothing happens. I have become the unknown stranger, the one the teacher told me to stay away from.

Finally, a young man stops—but far, far down the road. He yells from a safe distance, **You out of gas?" Slowly he comes closer. After creeping up to a safe talking distance, we negotiate. I give him five dollars for the gas and five dollars for his trouble.

After a full hour the young man has not returned with the gas. Out of desperation, I looked around and saw a white farmhouse about half a mile off. Crawling under a barbed wire fence and stepping across a creek, I walked along a farm road and found an elderly lady playing with some grandchildren in the rear of the house.

"I need gas for my car," I pleaded. She went immediately into the house, and in less than a minute three men came out. One went to the garage, another to a pickup, and a third was checking on fuel in a tractor.

Soon the older son and I drove off with an empty five-gallon can. After buying the gas for me at a nearby station, he drove back to my car where he poured the fuel into my tank. I offered him money but he refused, saying emphatically, "If anybody needs my help, nothing will stop me from giving it"

The son was imbued with the good-acting spirit of the mom and was carrying it into the world of which I was a part. The goodness power would not succumb to the fear that paralyzed the flow of goodness of thousands who passed by on the road. That day goodness had been intimidated by the fears of so many.

* * *

However, consider another highway, Interstate 90, running through Montana on across North Dakota. My heavy Cadillac went up a small hill doing seventy. Reaching the top, it seemed to be suspended in mid-air, then the front end crashed down with a hard thud. The motor was running but the car wasn't moving. Slowly it rolled down the hill, coasted to the bottom, and stopped. There I sat, in total darkness. I was in need for help.

Suddenly, after about five minutes of worry, I could see the flicker of a light behind me. I got out of the car and stood next to it as a vehicle approached. I could see it was a very small car as it came to a stop. It was the very first car, and it was almost midnight. "Someone was surely taking a risk for me," I thought.

Furthermore, inside the car was a family consisting of a husband, a wife, and two children. I explained my predicament. Quickly the mother squeezed the two children in with her in the back seat. She took my large piece of luggage and somehow squeezed that also in the back, allowing me to sit in the passenger seat.

I felt special. They brought me to their home in Glendive, where they made several calls. We were able to get a wrecker to tow the car that evening. The wife called various motels, getting the cheapest rates possible. They made arrangements to have the car brought to a repair garage, to provide a car for me to use in the morning, and to drive me to the motel. I had a goodness afterglow. I will remember this experience of caring forever.

There were two highways, two entirely different experiences. But there was a same experience too. The genuine process of doing a good act consisted of three steps:

1. Perception of power: In both incidents there is a perception of a stronger and a weaker party. Then comes in a balancing, the capable taking care of the less capable.

2. Decision to give: The decision is made to do a good act to benefit the victim rather than take advantage of the situation for another purpose.

3. Decision to accept risk: A decision is made that the amount of risk and the degree of inconvenience is acceptable.

It Doesn't Matter How Smart You Are If You Are Not Good

He comes with a price, forty-five dollars an hour. He comes with a reputation, a very good mechanic. You call him "my mechanic" and would even wish to invite him over for dinner. Clearly, you have considerable faith and satisfaction in your mechanic. Then, suddenly, that faith is ruined.

You brought your car in for a repair. Leaving the car you told him, "I'll be back in two hours." You returned in one hour. The car was washed and ready to go. But on the bill was a two-hour charge, ninety dollars for labor. The mechanic expected you to arrive in two hours. He did one hour of work and deliberately charged for two.

This mechanic was indeed smart. He was skilled in his trade, but that did not matter if he was not also good. He traded the good image of himself for a paltry forty-five dollars, and he reaped the scourge of distrust. Though he may be the best mechanic in the world, he will be judged ultimately more by the nature and quality of his goodness.

Indeed, intelligence, talents, and skills: all this may fall by the wayside if one fails to also be good. Nothing will impede the reciprocal flow of goodness between two people more than the exposed lie.

Because You Succeed Doesn't Mean You Intended to Be Good

Three men were each faced with a similar, perilous act, saving a drowning boy. All three did good acts because the outcome was successful. Success, in this case, equals a good act

It may make a difference to know that rescuer #1 did not mainly intend to save the boy. His main concern was to impress his girlfriend. Rescuer #2 did not, primarily, intend to save the boy either. He saw it as an opportunity of getting the boy's rich uncle to recommend him for a job. Rescuer #3 had a different focus. His primary objective was to save the boy because he believed it was right. Therefore, in your daily meandering, look for the likes of rescuer #3. With love he will serve you unconditionally. That caring hand that turns the barren sod, with love becomes the Hand of God.

The Menacing Power Struggle

A struggle between wills of a child and her mother, to see who will win the upper hand, is hardly perceived as a struggle aimed at achieving a good act.

"Kylee, sit here."

"Nooo, I want to look around."

"I'll count to ten, and I mean it."

"Nooo, noo."

"One, two..."

"I want a book to look at."

"It's time out for you. For not listening, you sit without a book."

"No, no," she starts crying.

"Kylee, stop it. You're too loud. I mean it. I will count to ten—one, two, three—You are asking for a spanking. I'm going to the ladies' room now." Kylee stumbles along, following her mother, sobbing.

The mother had a wonderful opportunity to perform a good act by allowing the child to have a book to look at. Her need to be right, her need for power seemed more persistent.

The Good Act Is Reserved Only for Those Who Deserve It

I was standing at the end of a line, about to get on a bus. "Why me?" I asked myself, being nudged by a stranger drinking water from a gallon container. It was all the luggage he had. He talked to me, and I listened patiently. I learned he had "loads" of children and a wife worth "twenty million" in San Diego. In the hustle of getting on the bus I lost track of Joshua, the name he gave. I was sort of glad he disappeared. I sat in the seat next to the last. My wife sat in front. Just as I pulled my cap down over my eyes I heard a "hi!" Across from me sat Joshua. He wanted my ear. So I listened: "New York was a trap, and the police were bigoted."

He wanted to converse with Steve, who sat in the seat in front of him. Intermittently, Joshua drank from the gallon container. He spat on the seat next to him. He opened and closed a cigarette pack he held in one hand, and in the other he flicked the lid of his lighter on and off.

I noticed for the first time that Joshua had a magazine. I asked to see it. "Why?" he blurted out. "Everybody should be dead—food eaters and old people—want me to break your neck?"

"Why do you treat me like that?" I asked, looking him squarely in the face. "I treat you with respect and kindness; you shouldn't treat mc like that." Then I turned, pulled my cap over my eyes, and tried to sleep.

I was fairly comfortable when I felt a nudge on my right shoulder. It was Joshua handing the magazine to me. There seemed to be a kind feeling tone in that act, like he was feeling guilty. Steve was within ear-shot of Joshua. Evasively, Steve struck up a conversation with another passenger. Joshua decided to listen in and randomly interject remarks. Steve suddenly moved to join the other conversant, leaving Joshua alone.

The bus stopped and three additional persons came aboard. Steve invited two to sit in his seats. Joshua, feeling he had to explore new territory in the front of the bus, gave up his seats to the third person, who plunged heavily into the seat Joshua had been spitting on.

Cigarettes and lighter in hand, Joshua sat with some other passengers in front. Eventually he was warned that his talking was unbearable to others, and he should cease or else leave the bus. The bus made three stops before reaching Memphis. In each case Joshua was the first to be out the door. In addition to lighting up, he sought out others. Those he approached felt compelled to walk away.

My wife and I had never taken the bus to Memphis before. When Steve learned that our destination was the John Hacke hotel, T was most surprised that he called someone on his cellular phone, then told us that he had arranged a cab service for us. He said generously, "It's all free."

We finally arrived at our destination. My wife, Steve, Joshua, and I were standing together. Joshua asked me for a quarter.

I gave Joshua 20 dollars. Then I handed him a pin. It read, "I am a good person." I pinned it on him as he requested. We shook hands, and Joshua returned to the bus.

Astonished at what he had seen, Steve declared, "He's the last person in the world I would give anything to, that obnoxious jerk."

"Neither would anybody else," I replied. "Joshua doesn't deserve it, but he needs it.

But now my wife and I were about to have a great surprise. It was that cab service. It had arrived in the form of Steve's wife, Nadine.

Steve was driven by an unbridled goodness impulse. Since we were newcomers, Steve wanted us to have a little tour. Finally, we came to our destination. Just before he left I put into his hand the same kind of pin I gave to Joshua.

The same pin had different meanings to the two who received it. To Joshua it represented a goal to aim for; to Steve it was a reminder of who he was.

The Spiral, a Menace to the Flow of God's Goodness

I have been hearing some news about throwaways, unwanted kids, 175,000 of them. What a deal! You don't want your kid who is at the rebellious age of sixteen or seventeen, and you lock him or her out, assuring the kid a bed under the freeway or in a dump. Incredible!

Unhappiness circles begin like this: She says, "Your feet are too big."

He replies: "Your toes are crooked."

"—And your relatives are uncivilized baboons."

"Your uncle chases one-legged roosters."

As you can see, it can spiral out of control and even turn violent. It can end before it starts, however, with—"Your are so right. My feet are the size of a baseball field"—and the spiral is gone.

I believe the unhappiness circle begins and spirals out of control with throwaway kids. Anger feeds on itself and accelerates to physical abuse. Parents insist they are right, and children say "blow it out of your ears" because the relationship is shot. Finally, with the authority residing with the parents, the kids earn the wages of war and maybe die, chewed up by the decadence of street life.

The Unhappiness Spiral—a destroyer of relationships, families, and nations—is just about the worst obstacle to the flow of God's goodness.

The Fruit of Goodness Is Dignity, Respect, and Compassion

Life seems to have its vacillations. Though you would like to be respected because you are good enough and deserving, you may be snubbed by the rules.

You are on a bus. Because you don't have the correct change you are left off at the next corner, far from your destination, until you find the correct change. That is the rule.

My third-grade teacher had a rule, really. If your handwriting was not acceptable she would strike your knuckles with a pointer. To this day I do not understand how that would improve handwriting.

The circus came to town, and a line formed at the men's bathroom. You stand in line and take your turn; that is the unwritten rule. Standing in that line I saw a young boy running in a circle. He couldn't stop moving, or else he would wet. Quickly I yanked him into a stall ahead of the others. He was last as far as the rule was concerned, and I put him first as far as his dignity was concerned.

Honesty may be a kind of rule. Cheating on a test violates that rule. It is serious because it represents a deception of self. If you falsely look great on a test, then you are not what you portray yourself to be.

A simple rule for right and wrong is based on role reversal. Just put yourself in the other person's place. Empathy is the word. It means to have the ability to feel not only for, but with someone. Try it. You might even feel comfortable violating some impersonal, unyielding rule.

The Urgency to Be Noticed

Ever since our first cry as a newborn we are yearning for attention. As an integral part of our being that we need to be noticed and appreciated for our goodness throughout life. If you have a person who will interact with you daily in a caring manner, then you can feel satisfied that you are noticed.

How you are noticed by others may be a reflection of your own expectations. They see you as handsome or pretty; you check it out by seeing heads turn. Now you are more cognizant of how you dress, walk, or smile because you like what's happening.

You may work for years in a medical lab and discover a cure for a disease. You now have the attention of a grateful populous. You have reinforced your notice with a prestigious award.

Or you may take another course, like Luke Helder, the young pipe-bomb suspect who confessed to planting eighteen pipe bombs in rural mailboxes. The best explanation offered by his Dad was, "He needed a little attention."

If you feel in need of attention, there is an answer. Pause from your daily routine for a moment, speak to God, and realize:

> *The Lord is standing next to yon,*
> *So close you both can touch—*
> *He likes knowing how you feel*
> *Cause he loves you very much.*

IX
Living by the Power of Goodness

A Goodness Lesson to Live By

The bowling alley on the left side had a gutter-fill for the small children. The alley on the right had no gutter-fill. Those eight years old and older used that alley. Eight-year-old Andy had his name written down for the right alley. Right off, Andy displayed a knack for the game. He could hold the ball high like the big persons, and he could let it go, but not so powerfully. He was an ace in wrist turning. All Andy needed was a circular alley to adjust to his bowling twist. Since the alley was not shaped like an arc, that ghastly gutter kept getting in the way.

Frequently Andy looked up at the scores, and over and over he slapped his knee in utter disgust. Beside the line next to the letter A, for Andy, were zeroes. Help to hold the ball, help to throw the ball bore no fruit. Andy put the ball on the alley and pushed it in the gutter with no twist, no effort. The ball went halfway and held there, needing a mid-lane retrieval. Andy looked at the racks of bowling balls instead of taking his turn, saying, "Let's go home. This place sucks."

Then Grandpa took Andy's turn. Five pins went down. Andy turned around. Suddenly a 5 appeared in his string of zeroes. We were a team. Reluctantly Andy dragged himself to the bowling ball return.

Looking at the five-point gain for some kind of self-redemption, he threw the ball with meaning. It was a twister that guttered like many before. It went in the gutter almost half way. "You went 6 feet before; now it's 16 feet. Wow!" Grandpa said, giving the boy a hug.

You cannot win without trying. You try to learn how to be better, better today than you were yesterday. If you challenge yourself before you challenge others, you will be better prepared for winning. Concentrate on developing your abilities first; the rest will follow.

How Good Is a Good Act?

A man with a black beard and three suitcases requested that the teller watch his luggage so that he could return with his car. The teller gave the man no reassurance, reminding him that it would be entirely at his own risk.

The conversation was overheard by a stranger. Like a guardian angel, he was overseeing the bearded man's property. It was twenty minutes later that the owner of the luggage appeared. "I was watching your luggage," he told him. The man's "thank you" was effusive, and his expression was one of disbelief as the stranger walked off. On a scale from 1 to 10, how good was the good act of the stranger?

Now, imagine a person approaching you, seeking information. You raise your arm and point, "That way." On a scale from 1 to 10, how good was your good act?

Suppose you responded differently as, "I'll show you exactly where you want to go. Come with me."

On a scale from 1 to 10, how good was this act? The second response probably has a higher good act rating. The help was more specific, more personal, and it involved sacrifice. The help involved a joy or willingness to assist that facilitated the contact. The person helped could easily feel special.

Life is such that you can stand, sit, or lie down, or you can move. Today you can add birdseed to your life, and tomorrow you can watch a bird show. Indeed, the more important you make something or someone else, the more you reap the goodness of your own giving.

Let the Good in You Be Your Guide

I have never been drunk because I do not drink. I think that surprises some who say, "Not even a little?" Others are uncomfortable because they find out that I will not be a drinking buddy. I cannot tell you how many times I have heard, "You don't drink?" It is like you're suddenly discovered to be a Martian.

There is a tradition at a wedding where, at some point, you are expected to drink to a toast. At one wedding in particular I did do the toasting along with everyone else. But my glass was empty. Those with keen eyesight, who enjoyed drinking most, picked up on my pretense. "Be a man. Have a drink," one invited me, reaching across the table and filling up my glass. 1 left the wedding reception with that ignoble "less than a man" designation intact. But it didn't bother me. I just counted on my fingers: one, two, three, four, five, six kids.

There is a little town in South Dakota surrounded by farmland. It had one bank, one grocery store, one church, one post office, and five saloons. Now and then I would happen to go in for a Pepsi.

One time, a farmer was sitting at the bar. "C'mere," he said, "I want to buy you a drink."

"No thank you," I replied, "I don't drink." He asked again for me to join him. Again, I declined.

"What do you have against farmers?" he slurred.

I don't drink because I don't like the taste of it. Furthermore, I would just fall asleep if I drank. It would take the fun out of me. I would be a quiet, anesthetized guy sitting in the comer or sleeping with the wall holding me up. I can't see anybody being happy to see me that way. Life is too short, and when you get older, life gets even shorter. You need a fresh head and a clear mind to express the goodness of God. If I can't walk straight, I'll miss my path; if I can't see straight, I'll miss my target Besides, my woman would box my ears.

Teaching Someone the Good I Know

I was using a copying machine. Sheets were coming out one at a time. Tim was there with his mother. Being curious, he slowly crept toward the machine. "Get away from there," his mother yelled in a stem voice. Tim bent over and looked to see where the papers were coming from and was immediately yanked away. "I told you, stand here," his mother ordered. Tim pulled away in a gesture of defiance.

"That's one I owe you—and I don't forget," the mother threatened.

I took Tim by the hand and pointed to the red button. The papers had stopped going through. He pressed the button and the papers started again. The mother was watching. I took the papers out and gave them to Tim, showing him where they should be piled. In a moment he was doing the job for me, pressing the red button and sorting the printed sheets of paper. Needless to say, the expression on his face was a happy one. His mother, who continued to watch carefully, said, "You made his day."

I saw what Tim needed. He didn't need to be frustrated and threatened. Instead, he needed a liberating, good act to appease his curiosity. What transpired was simple. I obeyed him in what he was asking, yet he never said a word to me. Yes, Tim was only five. I was old enough to be his Grandpa, and I listened to him. For that moment I was called.

When One Is Chosen: the Calling

Being good helps to restrain the worst in other people. It can be a healer. It can help mend differences. It can help someone to think well of you, and your good act can even elicit a favor. A good act can touch deeply; it can make another person cry out with joy. It can help us appreciate the good in others, recognizing that we are more alike than we are different. All of these are shared blessings of being good. Aristotle said, "We are good in order to be happy."

It was getting cold. As long as I am walking I can survive both the cold and my back pain well. By stopping I am victim to both. To find a pair of gloves would help, so I went in a store. I needed gloves to keep my hands warm. I headed over to the clothing section.

Suddenly, I noticed on the floor three sets of shoes, scattered about. Apparently someone tried them on and forgot to place them back on the shelf. Despite my pain I waited and watched to see who might feel inclined to pick them up off the floor. People looked down at them and walked on, stepping over them or kicking them. It was up to me to do it, I thought My spine would not allow me to bend over. Slowly, I went straight down on one knee. People stopped to look at me as I picked up one shoe, then another, and another. I placed all three pairs together neatly on the shelf where they belonged. Then, holding on to the shoe rack, I pulled myself up.

"Thank you, Lord, for choosing me to do a kindness," I said prayerfully. In my shape there didn't seem to be many kind acts left in me. I was happy because I was given the opportunity. Someone just crossed out everyone else and pointed a finger at me. Indeed, those who were watching me could rapidly place one leg in front of die other and painlessly bend over in a second to do what required minutes for me.

Whatever life's situation may be, to know you are chosen out of so many who are called is about the most powerful reason in the world to do good.

Where My Bait Lands, I Land

I am cast somewhere for a reason. It is no accident where I land this day; I land for a reason. I have the bait. Let me be prepared for the world to take it

I'm seeing an old lady, I mean really old, about ninety-five. She has a cane in one hand, and a little girl is holding her other arm. Her slowness tells me that she can barely function. She's passing by at the far side of the aisle. God, I hope she doesn't come over. With my luck she'll fall over and crush my sublime card creations with her frail body, and we'll have to call the ambulance, and the little girl will be crying.

Oh, no, she has read my mind. That stiff, age-wracked woman is stopped about ten feet away from my table. She lifts her cane and points at a card. It is the only romance card with big letters. She comes closer. With her arm trembling, her vein-bulging hand picks up the card.

"How much is this one?" she asks.

"It's free. Now if you buy a packet, consisting of five cards, that will be S4.95. One card is free. It's my policy."

I insert the card in an envelope and handed it to my last customer for the day. The fragile woman turns to the girl, who dutifully holds her one arm so she will not topple over, and said, "Grandpa will like this one." She read:

You are my first, and you are the best,
I chose only you, forsaking the rest.
You are my future; you are my past.
I promise you truly, you are my last.

As she shuffles away slowly I hear the old woman say to the little girl, "This one is better than the other one we took last week to grandpa's grave. And to think I almost stayed home today."

Where my bait lands, I land.
I am cast there for a reason.
Let me gladly give the bait
And be prepared for the world to take it.

God's Goodness Flows at Any Age

Some summers ago a group of elderly folks consented to come together to discuss the outflow of their goodness. Gladys, seventy-five, said somewhat proudly, "I had gone to the orchard yesterday to pick green apples for my friend." All Howard, seventy-nine, could think of was work. He was a volunteer church worker contributing four hours a day doing carpentry and lawn mowing. Years ago, Joan, eighty, remembered having taken a boy into their home who was locked out of his house and had no place to go. Christopher, eighty-one, a former baseball coach, remembered how he interceded when a dad berated his son who missed a fly ball.

Helen, eighty-four, stated, "I feel very uncomfortable bragging about the things I do. As a little girl, if I tooted my own horn, my mother would give me five times more work to do. I never received praise. I suppose that stayed with me until this day. Want to hear something funny?" Helen continued, '1 noticed this bottle on the sidewalk, smashed, with rough edges. I went inside and asked the clerk, 'Give me a broom and a pan, and I'll go out and pick up that bottle.'

"He looked at me—then he went and got me a dustpan and broom and passed it over the counter to me. The other clerk saw it and said to me, *What are you doing, going to take a ride?'"

Goodness Unifies

There is something about obedience that brings people together. Take a bunch of cars piling up in one place on the street. They surely look like they are obeying something. Sure enough, there is a light there. It is red, and they have stopped to follow a rule. The rule says a car stops on red. People follow it because it is a good safety feature. That is a rule made by people.

Mr. Jones gives ten dollars to a poor lady on the street There is a spiritual rule here, obeying the written word, "Help the poor," "Do unto others what you want them to do unto you," or "Love your neighbor as thyself."

Mr. Smith sees what Mr. Jones just did. Not to be outdone, he finds a poor man and gives him twenty dollars, twice as much as Mr. Jones gave to the poor lady. Mr. Smith follows the comparison rule. Compare yourself with your neighbor, look classier, prove to others that you have more goodness in you than Mr. Jones.

Jones is obeying the words of a Higher Power, while Smith is defending his own inadequacy by using the comparison method to gain satisfaction. All of us are somewhat like Mr. Smith. We want to show the good side of ourselves only, but we hide the back alley side of ourselves. We know which side the approval is on.

Believe it or not, both men can come together if one is willing to make a move. For Jones to become competitive, like Smith, is clearly not the correct move to make because the rivalry will intensify. Rather, Mr. Smith needs to relinquish to Mr. Jones the belief that goodness-giving—which is selfless—comes more reliably from obedience to a higher power. Now both can have the same reason for being good. Such obedience eliminates all self-serving reasons for being good and takes goodness from the level of man's ego desires and man's self-satisfactions and places it under the jurisdiction of God.

Look at the new scenario: Smith sees Jones giving the poor lady ten dollars. He says, "I want to be like Jones. I will give twenty dollars to a poor person." Smith does not compete, he is not envious; instead he emulates. That means he want to do like Jones. He is so impressed by the goodness of Jones that he wants to duplicate it, or even do better. Now both men are synchronized. They are not only adding goodness upon goodness, they discovered a commonality that binds them together.

When either Jones or Smith does a good act in the future there will be no trace of jealousy or rivalry. They will both be working for God. They will base their goodness-giving on the simple proclamation that every person exists in the image of God. Therefore, all human beings deserve to be treated with respect, dignity, and great value.

Oneness of Home and Country

Two teams, Arizona and New York, batted in the World Series, struggling to defeat one another. There was no compromising in it, no giving a break to the opposing side. But on the back of each uniform, just below the neckline, there was a symbol. A small American flag was sewn there. Though two teams were involved, distinct and separate, from different parts of the country, they had something in common.

I have a short wife whom I adore. She likes to put the canned food closer to the bottom of the pantry, near the floor. 1 don't like them there, so I take an inventory, "Hmmm, there are about three things I would like today, except I have to bend down, almost to floor level," I said to her. "Did you consider what arrangement would please your Sweetheart?"

She laughs at that. Again I remind her, "I am taller, and I prefer my canned goods at eye level."

As in the competitiveness of sports, differences are abundantly present in a marriage. But there is a serious side, a time when both must wear the same flag, representing the family. In protecting the integrity of the family, all those challenging, often petty differences, become inconsequential.

The glue in a family, and in a country as well, is enhanced by an adherence to a spiritual belief system. To encounter a serious threat is to turn to spirituality for protection, comfort, and hope. Perhaps that explains the recent, significant rise in the purchase of Bibles following the Twin 'lower tragedies.

When encountering a serious threat to a marriage, you've got to clutch at something strong.

If you are for God, then be unified with God. Speak with commonality. If you cannot clutch at that which unifies in a relationship then you may turn into driftwood, with no direction.

Let Fun Be Part of the Good You Do

The Laugh Doctor came to town. At Point Clear, Alabama, I saw him perform. Many people were in the crowd when he entered the large ballroom. He divided the crowd into three parts, the tee-hees, the ha-has, and the guffaws.

He put on his artificial nose and white wig and carried a symphony director's baton. He pointed to the left and heard tee-hee, tee-hee; he pointed to the middle and he heard ha-ha, ha-ha. He pointed to the right where he heard a raucous guffaw, guffaw. Then he blended them together again and again into a massive crescendo of laughter.

"Laughter is good for the soul," he said. The Laugh Doctor called us not human beings but humor beings, and he told us that we should smile more. We subsequently moved right ahead with smile exercises. "You lift your eyebrow up to your hairline," he instructed. I failed. My hairline was at the back of my neck. "Then you bend your head so your ear touches your shoulder.

"What was that cracking noise?

'Then you get your fingers and put them in at the corners of your mouth and stretch those lips." When all the teeth came to view, he said, " Hold it. Now turn to your neighbor."

Your neighbor looks and you look at a skull full of protruding teeth, and you both laugh yourselves silly.

But I admired that Laugh Doctor. Privately, I said to him, "You are good! 1 wish I could talk as fast as you—and you whiz around like a hummingbird. These jokes you tell keep people laughing," I said, "but I can't do that. You have a wonderful gift"

He smiled at me and said, "There is humor in everything we do. You can't stop the cold from its biting, you can't stop the gloominess of the sky, but you can impose humor on yourself at any time. You can have fun in frivolous places," he continued, "and you can have fun in serious places. Look in the mirror. Who do you see?" he asked. "I am you, and you are me. We both have gifts. What you can do I cannot do. But we are the same because we have the same Maker."

Gosh, I was surprised. We had never met before, and there he was, thinking a lot like me. The Laugh Doctor believed firmly that we should do the good we do with joy. That was the beautiful message he left me with, "Don't forget to have fun in everything you do."

We showered each other with our own complimentary, feel-good acts of being positive and uplifting. We had no rivalry and no jealousy, but we did have unity. Though we had different gifts to share, we were the same, one under God—just as it is written: "When two or more come together in my name, I am in their midst."

The Goodness of Caring Through Sharing

Caring is best when expressed not in wishes, but in sharing. It is probably less important what is shared than what impact the sharing will have on a relationship. If it is intended to elevate, to give value, to communicate liking and loving, and to foster closeness, then it serves to enrich and give meaning to the bond between two people.

What sort of transaction do we need between a couple to call the sharing significant? It depends on the status of the relationship. For a man and a woman going together, the sharing of a squeeze of a hand can have more significance than the exchange of expensive gifts.

One summer the first blueberry to ripen in my garden was a significant event. I made it significant. I fussed over it by deciding to give it to my sweetheart, yelling to her, "Honey, honey—look what I have for you." In my mind she should have it all. But in her mind, she wouldn't take it all. Carefully, she cut it in half. It was not a house or a car or expensive jewelry; it was a tiny, ripe blueberry, many of which you could eat by the handful and not give a second thought

But we were both focusing on a single blueberry. It may have never happened, the magic of that sharing moment. But no, for us it was fanciful and useful, engaging and uplifting. We were dancing, frolicking about something insignificant, and both feeling pleased with one another.

Sharing translates to caring. Emily, a granddaughter of mine, walked with me along a road in the mountains of North Carolina. She spotted wild blackberries growing alongside the road and decided to pick them. Her very first thought as she reached for the berries was, "Let's take some home to Grandma."

Imagine, four years old and already working on the idea of being good to people. Emily was about to make Grandma feel special through a simple act of sharing, and for that she would receive a hug, words of appreciation, being called a "good" girl, and a piece of Grandma's fresh apple pie. Even in her early age Emily realized that the best part of caring is the sharing.

Giving from a Need

The Aytas of Pinutubo are a tribe of people who are satisfied with having just the necessities of life: food, shelter, and clothing. Their focus is not in gaining abundance but in directing energies to caring, sharing, and helping others. They represent a model of goodness unsurpassed by a social group. Because they give of their own need, they touch the heart of others in a sacrificial, compassionate, unforgettable way.

The Aytas, who are barely four feet tall, can speak three languages, including English. They utilize the wisdom of the elderly as teachers for the young. Children are never physically punished but are frequently reminded of a god who may be displeased. The Aytas believe in good and evil and perform rituals where, regardless of the length of the performance, good inevitably triumphs. Thus they make themselves feel better with the reassurance that the crops will flourish or the sick will get well. They are honest and do not steal because their emphasis is not in achieving abundance but in being contented with just enough.

How Many Sides Does a Person Have?

Flip Wilson, the comedian, often said, "What you see is what you get." But there is a half you don't see. The hidden side prefers to be kept hidden. It shows up in such unexpected places and can affect the course of your life.

The two sides of yourself are all you've got, the good side and the hidden side. That is you, the total person. "You are wonderful, but so disgusting." We are talking about the same person. There is no contradiction. It is just a question of which side you are describing, the storefront or the back alley.

Sometimes you have a flip-flop, having the back-alley side show at least momentarily, pushing the good to one side. Living together long enough with someone can reveal it. Injustice can encourage it. As examples, road rage is a flip-flop, spousal abuse is a flip-flop.

Choosing a mate who is a good fit, whatever the particulars, is part of that process of selecting die best. Some imperfections arc a nuisance, but adjustments can be made. However, some back-alley sides are difficult to compromise and can trigger a divorce option.

You saw him and described him: "How wonderful you are. You are helpful, kind, and generous. I love your cute dimples, your humor, and your gentleness." If he will remain as you have described him for the first twenty years of marriage, then a mild, hidden side that emerges, like dropping his drawers on the floor, can be easily tolerated.

If you mean a great deal to someone, you can stand to be your total self because you won't be turned away. It is the expressions of goodness, the giving of it, and the taking of it that lightens the burdens and brightens one's day.

How much are you worth in the marketplace if your back-alley side and its imperfections are known? How much less are you then wanted and needed?

There is One who has already counted the hairs on your head, so completely are you known. The state of unconditional love is with you on the mountain and by the sea, in the forest or wherever you may be. It is the wonderful gift of God who knew you even before you were.

The Guardian Angel

The provisions of everyday living, like a car, a home, clothing, and medicines certainly make our existence pleasant But where do they come from?

If I said they come from a guardian angel you might be surprised. Persons you do not know developed creatively the many efficient items that contributed to your welfare and comfort. Indeed these are pioneers who have taken care of you, but they surely did not have you in mind. Yet, they have done many good acts for you. But all that would be in vain if the achievements were not available to possess.

Because our guardian angels are everywhere, we become less aware that they take care of us daily.

A guardian angel, rather than walking away, may deliberately wait longer to obey.

I was about to enter the post office. Diverting me was the sight of a tow truck backing up behind a white car. The owner of the car was an elderly woman, obese, gray-haired, and holding a cane.

"Having trouble?" I asked her.

"This is the second flat tire I had in thirteen years."

"Not bad," I remarked. "Being in town is a good place to have a flat—rather than on a farm road somewhere."

Quickly the tow man hoisted the rear of the woman's car about six inches off the ground. Now he was ready to tow. The situation seemed well in hand. The woman would ride with the man in the truck to the station.

Patiently I waited to obey if the circumstances would allow me. If they would have spoken clearly and told me to leave, I would have been on my way.

This looked like it. "Let's go," the tow man called to the elderly woman. He opened the door of the tow truck for the woman to get in. Seeing the high step, she said, "I can't get up there, my knee won't bend."

Being intentionally available and the only other person present, I was the one the woman turned to and asked, "Give me a ride in your car?"

"Of course," I replied.

I followed the tow truck to the station. Then, while her car was being tended to, I drove an additional six blocks to her trailer park and brought her to her front door.

Her "God bless you" was precious. A guardian angel waits until all is well.

X
Manipulations of Goodness

Serving self is a fairly universal objective. It has many guises. In the competitive business world there is a vying to see who gets the better number or quality of good acts. A good act can be made of nothing or it can be embellished into a mountain of gold. You can manipulate a good act so that it means just the opposite of what was intended. Love can be called hate and hate can be turned into love to someone, somewhere.

There is no law against the use of the term "good." It is allowed to be used, abused, twisted, and turned about. In business someone finds "good" in anything. It helps make a sale.

A town had a Good Neighbor Day sponsored by the local bank. Someone decided to distribute 2,000 roses. It was someone who thought everyone needed a rose. The fact is nobody needed a rose. If each town resident received five gallons of gasoline, that would approach a bona fide need. Residents were recipients of a good act but not a need-fulfilling act. It was the bank's way, superficial as it was, to glorify itself as "good." And what does this "good" bank get for its rose? Good business.

Recently I spent some time in a hotel. The manager wished that I offer comments about the services provided, whether or not hotel staff, guest room, guest bath, and overall satisfaction had met my expectations. The hotel manager was looking for an acknowledgment of the goodness of his hotel's services.

But he was concerned about the status of his good only. Nobody told me what a wonderful guest I had been. Nobody acknowledged that I had had no wild part or that my TV was not blasting loudly. No, my good did not matter to the manager. "If you tell me how good I am as a guest, I will tell you how good you are as a manager," I said, surprising him. He reminded me that I was only the run-of-the-mill guest. But though I wanted him to tell me I was a "good one," he could not. Apparently, he decided that the embellishment of his "good image" was more important than the recognition of my "good image." He could not agree to reciprocate.

The Arbitrary Use of Good

Goodness can be anchored to a belief system such as a Christian tradition, or it can be relative. If it is relative then any act can be called good primarily to satisfy or gratify the ego. The ego makes excuses for itself and, therefore, chooses to be always right and free from blame. There is no accountability because right and wrong are not separated or distinguished except for the purpose of serving self. Using good in relative terms is to allow oneself to justify all behaviors by making excuses for them with a simple judgment: "I am always right."

If a parent considers goodness as relative, all a child's acts are defined according to the expectations of the parent. What is good for the parent should be good for the child. If a parent is annoyed with the presence of his own child, it is good that he should give the child what he wants so he is not an annoyance. The less contact with the parent, the more the child is considered as "good." "Children should be seen and not heard" may be a good concept for a parent to apply to this relationship. But let us go a step further and define the good child as one who should be neither seen nor heard.

The modem day technologies, such as computers, sophisticated toys, and cars are readily provided. The message is, "It is good to go there, not here. Be far away. I call that being a 'good' boy."

To John, the child, it is "good" to be rejected, unloved, and unwanted. Well, what does John do with such a portrait of himself? To his classmates, to belong, to be loved, or to be wanted is good, causing John to feel confused. His message is exactly the opposite.

Once John behaves as if he must be rejected, that makes it easier for the other children to fulfill his wish and reject him more and more. Finally, the whole world is a rejecting place. Then he explodes, kills others and himself, not unlike the Columbine incident. I don't think it was an act of revenge for not belonging or of jealousy but rather a confused act where he was demanding to be right. To be good was to be unwanted. "If I am unwanted and dispensable " he reasoned, "you should be unwanted and dispensable," hence the shooting, hence he has proven he is right. John was demonstrating that "my kind of good—rejection—is better than your kind of good—acceptance."

These are the times for violence to sell and flourish. These are the times when guns are used to settle disputes. These are the times when family life is the most unstable, incomplete, and dysfunctional. These are the times when the technological and socially regressive milieu has its special manner of destructive expression. School shootings are the manifestations of this socially regressive milieu.

A Down-on-Life Attitude

This is about a seventy-six-year-old retired psychiatrist. We were on the same plane, sitting next to each other. Irene didn't like Monet or Picasso. Mozart was for three-year-olds. Bach was okay in places, but Beethoven was the greatest Contemporary art was ridiculous. "I live by common sense," she pointed out "I am analytical."

Taking note of her age, I asked her about the hereafter. She replied, "Who cares? I don't think about it. Religion was not a part of my upbringing."

"Would you accept a prayer?" I asked.

"I would appreciate that. It would be a compliment, that's all."

"What do you think of faith?"

"I'd rather have willpower. Where there's a will there's a way."

"—and suffering, what of suffering?"

"It has no purpose. Too much is too much. If people want to, let them die. Kavorkian is doing a wonderful job. I once gave a friend a high dose of medicine—dead the next morning.

"That Encyclical by the Pope, valuing life? Ridiculous. That time somebody shot him? They should have killed him. There are too many people in the world—and how many children do you have?"

"Six."

"That's irresponsible. You are disgusting. Why have a child if he or she is unwanted? Why?"

"But a child is precious, Irene."

Clearly disgusted, Irene turned to her book by George Bernard Shaw. Competitively, I pulled out a book also, Good Morning, Holy Spirit

Irene and I traveled to the same hotel in Baltimore where, in the foyer, I decided to give her a hug. "Don't misunderstand," she said,

"I think you are a nice person." It was a calling, but that was the best I could do.

The Go-Between

The Senior Citizens is a helping organization. It raises funds to provide Christmas baskets for shut-ins. It provides social programs for the elderly, assists in Meals on Wheels, visits the homebound, and provides transportation for those who need help.

There they were, a faithful half dozen, standing in freezing temperatures in front to the supermarket and attempting to sell their cookies. People would come, look, and sift through the bagged cookies. Slowly the big pile began to diminish. Having persons trade money for the merchandise offered was a business transaction.

"Here is five dollars for the Senior Citizens," one lady said, taking no bag of cookies. For this person the Senior Citizens and their goodness happened to be more important than the cookies.

The lady was addressing their need and the community's need. If everyone did the same, settling for a "thank you" instead of cookies, then the cookies would not be required. There would be no need for a go-between, the cookies, because the money would go directly to the need.

Suppose it was not possible for you to give to the Senior Citizens directly, but you knew of their work and wished to give them five dollars. Now as your go-between you would have The Senior Citizens' Humanitarian Fund. But this type of go-between has teeth; it chews on your five dollars. Now, maybe four dollars goes to your destination.

There are many different kinds of go-betweens, collecting agencies, that sandwich themselves between the needy person and the giver. The more sandwiching you do, the less money comes out of the pot for the intended needy. Thus, the power of God's goodness may be trickled down to a few cents on the dollar so that those who need more are given less.

Thou Shall Kill Thy Neighbor

I always thought that goodness, sacrifice, repentance, and love of God were requirements for getting to heaven. In the Ten Commandments it is taught, "Thou shalt not kill."

I must be missing something. All of a sudden killing is good. Someone somewhere made a vicious killing machine of God because now killing is a password to heaven.

Not only is our life shaken up by explosions and innocent people dying, but trying to understand it, we become totally befuddled. We don't understand: how could anyone believe so recklessly that human beings should die so another can become a martyr? Now we realize there is a belief system that actively pursues the killing of thousands and millions of people because they have different beliefs. Persons such as Bin Laden are thrusting confusion into our otherwise steadfast, logical, and compassionate minds.

But our goodness is at hand to overcome any contradictions and confusions facing us. Be as good as you are. Be an arm of the Goodness Brigade and watch all that Bin Laden confusion fade. The flow of God's goodness represents the most righteous right of all. Give your goodness to the world, to your friends and family, and see it touch even hearts unseen, remembering that with your goodness you will conquer evil.

Overcoming Fear

When I was a boy we had in our neighborhood a large tree. It was unusually shaped. As often as I passed that tree I gave it no thought. It was leafless. It had died and left its bare branches feeling for the sky.

An Aunt of mine, who thought she heard skeleton bones clicking under her bed, also discovered a strangeness about the tree—it was shaped like a witch. The word spread, and I began to examine that tree, wondering, "Could it be that it really looked like a witch?"

My imagination went wild. Soon I was walking backwards with my eyes shut as I passed that tree, which I had passed numerous times before without a twinge of fear. Other kids would just take the long way around the tree, and one boy blessed himself and ran for his life. Once I could have sworn those long, brambly arms came down swishing after me.

An inevitable characteristic of fear is that it becomes personalized. You will respond, as you may feel threatened. Fear is inescapable. Examples are, "I'm afraid because I lost my job," or "I'm afraid he doesn't love me anymore."

Fear is rational or irrational. It can cause a national hysteria. In view of the terrorism that potentially exists in the country there is cause for fear but probably not to the level of panic.

Fear is adjustable. It can be soothed by a friend, it can be stroked into a slight purring by the reassurance of a loved one, or it can—bombastically and frighteningly—scream at you like from a megaphone, enough to make you tremble and lose sleep. But there is a goodness that overcomes our fear.

Be Not Afraid

Speak of your fear to the wall or ceiling;
Speak to the floor or the chair;
Speak to the moon, the sun, and the summer—
God is everywhere.

Hear with your fear the wind at jour window;
Hear all the stirrings and whisperings of fright;
Then hear with your fear God's gentle voice
speaking,
'There, there my child, it will be all right."

See with your fear the great wonders of God
Who gives to darkness a light—
Now see with your fear that God is quite near
Then rest in His arms a good night.

"Soothing Gems"
Greeting card series by Phil Stack

Published by Tatay Jobo Elizes
My Book List - Contact:
job_elizes@yahoo.com - tatay@usa.com

My website - http://tinyurl.com/mj76ccq

Writings 1 Book, 2012 + + 1. Obit, *Bambi Harper* + + 2. Speech, UP, 2003, *Butch Jimenez* + + 3. Speech, Silliman U, 2006, *Butch Jimenez* + + 4. The Mission Moment, *Dr. Phil Stack* + + 5. Subanon Spirits of Rice & Land - *Noel Cornel Alegre* + + 6. I Look Out The Window - *Atty. Toto Causing* + + 7. Ride On A Bus, Poem, *Melanie Ferrer, et al* + + 8. Why Am I Doing This, *Susie Barbieri* + 9. How To Court A Philippine Lady, *Rodel Ramos, et al* + + 10. Story of Bacna Surgical Mission, *Sylvia Salvador* + + 11. Catch That Story, *Tatay Jobo Elizes*

Writings 2 Book, 2012 + + 1. There Is Hope For The Philippines, *Grace Padaca* + + 2. Pointers On Employment Abroad, *Melanie Aquino* + + 3. Without KNCHS: (Love story), *Atty. Toto Causing* + + 4. 422 Years Ago, *Rodel Rodis* + +5. Filipino American History Month, *Rodel Rodis* + + 6. A Need For Reflection, Gloom, *Cesar Torres* + + 7. Did Ninoy Die For Nothing, *Joey Concepcion* + + 8. Criteria - American Institute of Philanthropy, *Charity Guidelines (Feature)* + +9. Coming Revolution In The Ballot, *Cesar Lumba* + + 10. 2009, A Retrospective, *Cesar Lumba* + + 11. Strangers In Our Own Country, *Casiano Mayor Jr.* + + 12. The Gypsy Soul, *Casiano Mayor Jr.* + + 13. An End To Cheating, *Sonny Coloma* + + 14. Toward Culture of Giving, Not Having, *Sonny Coloma* + + 15. 100 Reasons to be Proud as Pinoys,*Anonymous*

Writings 3A Book, 2012 + +
1. EPIC25, Emerging Philippines Investors Coalition, *Norman Madrid* + + 2. Management Ability As An Issue, *Dr. Rene B. Azurin* + + 3. Do We Really Want To Give Our Politicos More Power, *Dr. Rene B. Azurin* + + 4. Will 2010 Fulfill Filipinos High Hopes For Better Life – Metamorphosis, *Ernie D. Delfin* + + 5. Comelec Is The Root Of All Evils, *Toto Causing* + + 6. Some Advantages of Federalism and Parliamentary Government For The Philippines, *Dr. Jose Abueva* + + 7. Sometimes A Great Nation, *Mar-Vic Cagurangan* + + 8. Great Conspiracy, *Mar-Vic Cagurangan* + + 9. Of Speech & Life's Riddles, *Casiano Mayor* + + 10. Bad Start To The Year, *Rod Garcia* + + 11. A Dinner out, *Rod Garcia* + + 12. One More Time, *Roy Gaane* + + 13. Strange Noises – *Tatay Jobo Elizes* + +

Writings 3B Book, 2012 + +
1. The Reeds and Beams of Sunset in Paite and Balangaging in

Candari + + 23. If You Dream It, Do It Retirement, *Cesar D. Candari +* + 24. Only In America, Human Interest Story, *Anonymous*

Writings 11 Book, August, 2011 + + 1. SONA In English and Filipino, *Pres. Benigno Aquino III (P-Noy)* + + 2. Telltale Signs: SONA and the Dogfight Over Spratlys, *Rodel Rodis* + + 3. Why China will not bring the Spratlys issue to the United Nations, *Ted Laguatan* + + 4. Random Thoughts, On Website Demise and On Disunity, *Tatay Jobo Elizes* + + 5. Can Local Private Sector Help Reverse Philippine's Migration Addiction?, *Jeremiah M. Opiniano* + + 6. What Fuels the Passion of Filipinos to Pursue Studies and Work in UK?, *Ofw Journalism Consortium* + + 7. Our Life in the Philippines, *Bob & Carol Hammerslag* + + 8. Reality Check: the Philippines – A Tropical Paradise for the Retiree?, *by Bob & Carol Hammerslag* + + 9. Filipinos Dominate Cruise Ships, *Roger P. Olivares* + + 10. Vargas: Hero, Villain, Tragic Figure?, *Roger P. Olivares* + + 11. Is it Hell to go Back Home?, *Roger P. Olivares* + + 12. The Filipino, now a commodity!, *Roger P. Olivares* + + 13. How US Can Create Jobs, *Rob Ceralvo* + + 14. Modus Operandi - Common Crimes (In Metro Manila, Philippines), *Anonymous* + + 15. Poem, Kabuhayang Bansa At Wika, *Irineo P. Goce (aka KaPule 2 and Leonidas Agbayani)* + + 16. Random Sayings & Advices, *Anonymous*

Writings 12 Book, April 2012 + + 1. Twenty Excuses Filipinos Use, *Orion Perez Dumdum* + + 2. One By One, The Petals Drop, *Julia C. Lagoc* + + 3. Religion & the Scientist, *Honorio M. Cruz, MD* + + 4. The Tales of the Aswang & Bangungot, *Honorio M. Cruz, MD* + + 5. Sex & Politics, *Honrio M. Cruz, MD* + + 6. Autopsy, *Ben Gonzales, MD* + + 7. Geekmocracy, *Mar-Vic Cagurangan* + + 8. Flights: Voice from the Future that Lives in the Past, *Mar-Vic Cagurangan* + + 9. Kaya Natin! Sanctuary, *Marisa Lerias* + + 10. The Days of Courage, *Gerry Partido* + + 11. Earth Day and the Tragedy of a Famous River, *Cesar D. Candari, MD, FCAP Emeritus* + + 12. Few Filipino-American NonprofitsGetting Political, *Erwin De Leon* + + 13. Filipino-American Political Invisibility And Community Organizations, *Erwin De Leon* I+ + 14. I'm 32 and I am still a Virgin, *Jovelyn Bayubay Revilla* + + 15. Hiding Ill-Gotten Wealth, *Jobo Elizes*

Writings 13 Book, July 2012 + +
1. From "Criminal" to "Doctor" in Criminal Justice, *Raymundo E. Narag* + + 2. The Essence of Giving, *MLMunoz* + + 3. My Prescription for Spiritual Life, *Sonja Barbara dL Munoz* + + 4. Anak Ng Prosti, *Pamela Joy Agtoto* + + 5. Ang Kapangyarihan ng Kanyang Pag-ibig, *Percival Campoamor Cruz* + + 6. Ang Tato ni Apo Pule, *Percival Campoamor Cruz* + + 7. Rapture, *Percival Campoamor Cruz* + + 8. Ang Taong Walang Anino, *Percival Campoamor Cruz* + + 9. Gender Formula – Boy or Girl, *Tatay Jobo Elizes* + + 10. The Single, *Jhackie Eslit Bayobay* + + 11. Why I Am Angry, *Jhackie Eslit Bayobay*, 12. Rules of Living, *Jhackie Eslit Bayobay* + + 13. Being Alone, *Jhackie Eslit Bayobay* + + 14. Love and Hurt, *Jhackie Eslit Bayobay* + + 15. My First Heart Aches, *Jhackie Eslit Bayobay* + + 16. Why the Philippines Need Sex Education, *Reygel Saplad Perales* + +

Timely Writings 14, 2013 + +

1The Giant Sucking Sound and the Rise of Employnomics, *Cesar Fernando Lumba* + + 2. UP, College of Bus. Admin. and Cesar E.A. Virata, *Eugenio Pulmano* + + 3. The Missing Element in Education Reform, *Late Sec. Jesse Robredo* + + 4. China: Some Observations from My Recent Trip, *Antonio Nievera* + + 5. Don't invest in stocks if you don't have these, *Alvin T. Tabanag* + + 6. Creating Your Own Financial Plan, *Alvin T. Tabanag* + + 7. Anti-Gay Hate Crimes on the Rise in New York City: A Call to the Community, *Kevin L. Nadal, Ph.D.* + + 8. Native Colonialism & Subjugation, *Anonymous (TJ Friend)* + + 9. The Way We Were - Fond Look at a Hometown, *Fred Natividad & Bing Castillo* + + 10. Obituary: Common Sense, *Anonymous* + + 11. Be The Best Ever, *Anonymous* + + 12. Remembering Capt. Rene N. Jarque, *Ellen Tordesillas* + + 13. Why I Left the Military, *Late Capt. Rene N. Jarque* + + 14. Soldiers In Elections: From Pawns to Knights, *Late Capt. Rene N. Jarque* + + 15. Reforming The Armed Forces - *Late Capt. Rene N. Jarque* + +

Timeless Writngs-15, May, 2014 + +
1 - Protecting the Nation's Marine Wealth in the West Philippine Sea, *By Supreme Court Justice Antonio T. Carpio* + + 2 – Are Filipinos United Against China's Invasion of Ayungin Shoal, *By Rodel Rodis* + + 3 – Telltale Signs: Why Are There So Many Nurses in the US? *By Rodel Rodis* + + 4 – Telltale signs: Philippines – A Jewish Refugee from the Holocaust, *By Rodel Rodis* + + 5 - Telltale Signs: OFW Remittances Promote Mendicant Culture, *By Rodel Rodis* + + 6 – Adding Insult To Injury: UP College Named After Marcos' Prime Minbister, *By Ted Laguatan* + + 7 - Aquino To Nation: "This Is Your SONA." *By President Benigno Aquino III* + + 8 – Why We Are Poor: A Purpose for the Middle Class, *By F. Sionil Jose* + + 9 - Secrets of a Romantic Man, *By Dr. Phil Stack* + + 10 - Totoong Buhay Sa Canada, *By Racz Kelly* + + 11 - Small Steps to Building a Nation, *By Bert Armada* + + 12 - The Rising of a Nation. *By bert Armada* + +

Timeless Writings Book – 16 , July 2014 + +
1. The Martyrs of Camarines Norte, *by the heirs* + + 2. The Self-Perpetuating Elite of the Philippines, *by Rodel Rodis* + + 3. Isang Open Letter Tungkol sa Trapiko, *by Ragulane* + + 4. Truest Yet Rendered Death Ode of Rizal by *Robert M. Bernardo, 2014* + + 5. Aquino SONA 2014: PNoy's 5th SONA Full Transcript (English version), *by Pres. Benigno Aquino III* .

Solo Authored Books: + + +

Book A, **Turning Points,** *Job Elizes Sr,1968 (Reissue 2009)* + + +
Book B, **Be Considerate For Once,** *Tatay Jobo Elizes (Jr), 2013*
Book C, **Piglets Unlimited - Wealth,** *Tatay Jobo Elizes, 2009* + + +
Book D, **Out of the Misty Sea We Must,** *Cesar Lumba, 2010* + + +
Book E, **Fulfilled** - *Gonzales Reynaldo, Editor, 2010* + + +

Dook F - **Reflections** - *Bert Guiang, 2010* + + +
Book G, **Writings 7 - My Vintage Pics,** *Tatay Jobo Elizes, 2010* +
Book H, **May Bagwis Ang Pag-ibig,** *Percival C. Cruz* + + +
Book I, **Letters To Matrimony,** *Irineo P. Goce, Ka Pule2, 2011* +
Book J, **Songs I Wish You Knew,** *Soledad R. Juan, 2011* + + +

Book K, **Make My Day,** *Larry Henares Jr., 1993, Re-issue 2011* +
Book L, **Our Guerrero Family,** *Tatay Jobo Elizes, 2010* + + +
Book M, **Handy Jokes,** *Tatay J. Elizes, 2011* +
Book N, **FaveArt 1,** *Tatay Jobo Elizes, 2011* + +
Book O, **Beyond idle thoughts,** *MLMunoz, Sept,2011* + + +

Book P, **Cracks In The Armor,** *Mariano Ngan, Oct 2011* + + +
Book Q, **FaveArt 2,** *Tatay Jobo Elizes, 2011* + +
Book R, **Balitang Kutsero,** *Perry Diaz, Jan 2012* + + +
Book S, **FaveArt3,** *Tatay Jobo, 2011* + + +
Book T, **FaveArt4** *,2012, Tatay Jobo* + + +

Book U, **Stack Family Journals,** *Phil & Fe Stack, 2012* + + +
Book V, **Emily, An Adoption Journey,** *Romerl Elizes, 2012* + + +
Book W, **Hermes Alegre Art Gallery,** *TJ & Hermes, 2012* + + +
Book X, **Masaya Din, Malungkot Din,** *Jovelyn B. Revilla, 2012*
Book Y, **Tiis, Sipag At Tiyaga,** *Raquel Delfin Padilla, 2012* + + +

Book Z, **Until I Meet You,** *Jhackie Eslit Bayobay, 2012* + + +
Book AA, **Buhay At Pag-ibig,** *Argel Lucero Tamayo, 2012* + + +
Book AB, **Hail to the Second Best,** *Dr. Philip Stack, 2012* + + +
Book AC, **Life Bus,** *Mommy Joyce Pineda-Faulmino, 2012* + + +
Book AD, **My Candid Musings,** *Monette Dioquino Calugay, 2012* +

Book AE, **Tickets to Life,** *Maria Lourdes Jesalva, 2012* + + +
Book AF, **The Dove Files,** *Mike Portes, 2012* + + +
Book AG, **Nursing Vignettes,** *Jocelyn Cerrudo Sese, 2012* +
Book AH, **Poor Ba Us,** *R.A. Gubalane, 2012* + + +
Book AI, **Summer Idyll,** *Avelina Gil, 2012* + +

Book AJ, **Legacy (Pamana),** *Rachel Astrero, 2012* + +
Book AK, **Narratives Old & New,** *Avelina J. Gil, 2013* + +
Book AL, **Buhay Saudi,** *Adele J. Esic, 2013* + +
Book AM, **Buhay Ofw Atbp,** *Jessica Napat, 2013* + +
Book AN, **Mga Tula Ng Buhay,** *Angelita C. Esguerra, 2013* +

Book AO, **Not by Bread Alone,** *Judge Lily V. Magtolis, 2013* +
Book AP, **Jokes Collection-2,** *Tatay Jobo Elizes, 2013* + + +
Book AR, *My Writings Sometimes, Tatay Jobo Elizes, 2013*
Book AS, **Sa 'Yo Na Ako,** *Shayne A. Martinez, 2013*
Book AT, **My Kin's Family Trees,** *Tatay Jobo Elizes, 2013*

Book AU, **Rizal Family Tree & Others,** *Tatay Jobo Elizes, 2013*
Book AV, **Make My Day-2, Nice & Nasty,** *L. Henares, 2013 (1993)*
Book AW, **Make My Day-3, Cecilia, Love,** *L.Henares, 2013 (1993)*
Book AX, **Handy Lyrics-1,** *Tatay Jobo Elizes, 2013*
Book AY, **Ang Biblos,** *Rev. Dr. Eugenio Guerrero, 2014 (1929)*

Book AZ, **Make My Day-4, Sweet & Sour,** *L. Henares, 2014 (1993)*
Book BA, **Life's Journey, True Stories,** *Dr. Phil Stack, 2014*
Book BB, **Gerry Gil Writings-1,** *Danny Gil, 2014*
Book BC, **Mr. President,** *Hermie Rotea, 2014*

Book BD, **Nostalgic Pics** *1, Tatay Jobo Elizes, 2014*

Book BE, **MakeMyDay-5, Saints & Sinners,** *Henares, 2014 (1993)*
Book BF, **MakeMyDay-6, Villains & Heroes,** *Henares, 2014 (1993)*
Book BG, **Nostalgic Pics 2 (ElizesClan),** *TatayJE, 2014*
Book BH, **MakeMyDay-7, Tough & Tender,** *Henares, 2014(1993)*
Book BI, **MakeMyDay-8, Light & Shadow,** *Henares, 2014(1993)*

Book BJ, **MakeMyDay-9, Give & Take,** *Henares, 2014(1993)*
Book BK, **MakeMyDay-10, ToBeOrNotToBe,** *Henares, 2014(1993)*
Book BL, **Emily Forever In Love,** *Emily Espanol Derry, 2013*
Book BM, **The Sinatra Songbook,** *Henares, 2014*
Book BN, **The Gaborro Reader,** *Allen Gaborro, 2010*

Book BO, Ramon H. Lopez - *Art Gallery, 2014*
Book BP, Philippines Via Old Pics-1, *Tatay Jobo, 2014*
Book BQ, Ronna Manansala - *Art Gallery, 2014*
Book BR, Philippines Via Old Pics-2, *Tatay Jobo, 2014*
Book BS, Being Good-A Medley Of Love, *Dr. Phil Stack, 2014*

Book BT, Lifestream Fisherman, A Fil.Odyssey, *Paul Dalde, Jul2014*

Please buy online or give as gift in paperback or kindle edition. All authors and titles are easy to search, trace or find online. Thanks. Self-Publisher, Tatay Jobo Elizes

Disclaimer: The Publisher disclaims liability over the author's words.

ISBN Code. Printed in the United States of America under ISBN codes below.
ISBN-13: 978 - **1500576752**   + + +   ISBN-10: **1500576751**

Publisher's - Contact job_elizes@yahoo.com, tatay@usa.com

My websites: http://tinyurl.com/mj76ccq + www.jobelizes.webs.com
"Buy A Book or Gift Somebody - paperback or kindle edition online"